Lecture Notes in Computer Science 7110

Commenced Publication in 1973
Founding and Former Series Editors:
Gerhard Goos, Juris Hartmanis, and Jan van Leeuwen

Yun Q. Shi (Ed.)

Transactions on Data Hiding and Multimedia Security VII

 Springer

Volume Editor

Yun Q. Shi
New Jersey Institute of Technology
University Heights, Newark, NJ 07102-1982, USA
E-mail: shi@njit.edu

ISSN 0302-9743 (LNCS)   e-ISSN 1611-3349 (LNCS)
ISSN 1864-3043 (TDHMS)   e-ISSN 1864-3051 (TDHMS)
ISBN 978-3-642-28692-6   e-ISBN 978-3-642-28693-3
DOI 10.1007/978-3-642-28693-3
Springer Heidelberg Dordrecht London New York

Library of Congress Control Number: Applied for

CR Subject Classification (1998): K.6.5, E.3, C.2, D.4.6, I.4, I.5

Typesetting: Camera-ready by author, data conversion by Scientific Publishing Services, Chennai, India

Printed on acid-free paper

Springer is part of Springer Science+Business Media (www.springer.com)

Preface

This issue contains seven papers. The first three papers deal with the protection of digital videos. In the first paper, Meerwald and Uhl describe an efficient and robust watermarking scheme integrated into the H.264/SVC video coding standard and address the coarse-grain quality and spatial resolution scalability features according to Annex G of the H.264 standard. In the second paper, Yamada et al. describe an improved system for embedding watermarks into video frames in real time using software running on an ordinary personal computer, which can be used for a parallel-computing platform. In the third paper, Echizen et al. describe a method based on infrared light that can prevent videos and movies displayed on a screen from being recorded with digital cameras and/or camcorders without authorization.

In the fourth paper a secure watermarking scheme for 3D geometric models is presented by Wu and Cheung, in which the independent component analysis and orthogonal transformation matrix are utilized. In the fifth paper, Cao and Kot measure the statistical correlation inconsistencies in mobile images for tamper detection. The last two papers are on steganography. In the sixth paper, Sur et al. present a secure steganographic method which involves randomized cropping. In the last paper, by Zhao et al., a steganographic scheme in streaming multimedia over networks is presented.

We hope that this issue is of great interest to the research community and will trigger new research in the field of data hiding and multimedia security. We want to thank all the authors and reviewers, who have devoted their valuable time to the success of this seventh issue. Special thank goes to Springer and Alfred Hofmann for their continuous support.

November 2011

Yun Q. Shi
(Editor-in-Chief)
Hyoung-Joong Kim
(Vice Editor-in-Chief)
Stefan Katzenbeisser
(Vice Editor-in-Chief)

Table of Contents

An Efficient Robust Watermarking Method Integrated in H.264/SVC

Peter Meerwald* and Andreas Uhl

Dept. of Computer Sciences, University of Salzburg,
Jakob-Haring-Str. 2, A-5020 Salzburg, Austria
{pmeerw,uhl}@cosy.sbg.ac.at
http://www.wavelab.at

Abstract. In this article we investigate robust watermarking integrated with H.264/SVC video coding and address coarse-grain quality and spatial resolution scalability features according to Annex G of the H.264 standard. We show that watermark embedding in the base layer of the video is insufficient to protect the decoded video content when enhancements layers are employed. The problem is mitigated by a propagation technique of the base layer watermark signal when encoding the enhancement layer. In case of spatial resolution scalability, the base layer watermark signal is upsampled to match the resolution of the enhancement layer data.

We demonstrate blind watermark detection in the full- and low-resolution decoded video for the same adapted H.264/SVC bitstream for copyright protection applications and, surprisingly, can report bit rate savings when extending the base layer watermark to the enhancement layer. Further, we consider watermark detection integrated in the H.264/SVC decoder operating on the partially decoded residual data for copy control or authentication applications.

Keywords: Robust watermarking, blind detection, H.264/SVC, scalable video coding.

1 Introduction

Distribution of video content has become ubiquitous and targets small, low-power mobile to high fidelity digital television devices. The Scalable Video Coding (SVC) extension of the H.264/MPEG-4 Advanced Video Coding standard describes a bit stream format which can efficiently encode video in multiple spatial and temporal resolutions at different quality levels [16,17]. Scalability features have already been present in previous MPEG video coding standards. They came, however, at a significant reduction in coding efficiency and increased coding complexity compared to non-scalable coding. H.264/SVC employs inter-layer prediction and can perform within 10% bit rate overhead for a two-layer resolution scalable bitstream compared to coding a single layer with H.264.

---

* Supported by Austrian Science Fund (FWF) project P19159-N13.

Y.Q. Shi (Ed.): Transactions on DHMS VII, LNCS 7110, pp. 1–14, 2012.

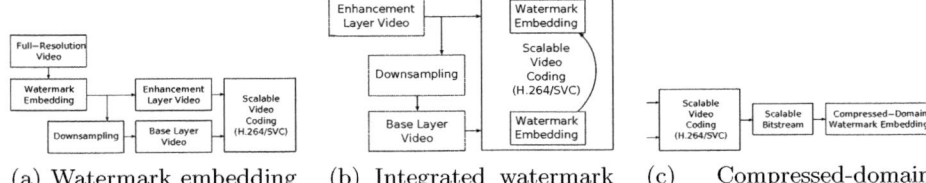

(a) Watermark embedding before video encoding

(b) Integrated watermark embedding and coding

(c) Compressed-domain embedding after encoding

Fig. 1. Different embedding scenarios for watermarking resolution-scalable H.264/SVC video content

In this work we investigate a well-known robust watermarking framework proposed by Noorkami et al. [11,12] for copyright protection and ownership verification applications of H.264-encoded video content. The aim is to provide a single scalable, watermarked bit stream which can be distributed to diverse clients without the need to re-encode the video material. Scalability is provided at the bit stream level. A bit stream with reduced quality, spatial and/or temporal resolution can be efficiently obtained by discarding NAL units [16]. The watermark (i) should be detectable in the compressed domain *and* the decoded video without reference to the original content, and (ii) must be detectable in the decoded video at all scalability operation points, starting from the base layer.

In Fig. 1 we distinguish three embedding scenarios for producing a watermarked, scalable H.264/SVC bitstream: (a) embedding before encoding, (b) embedding integrated in the coding process, (c) altering the scalable bit stream (embedding in the compressed domain). The first embedding scenario offers little control over the resulting bitstream and thus makes detection in the compressed domain difficult. As watermark embedding takes place before video encoding, any robust video watermarking schemes can be applied. However, lossy compression and downsampling of the full-resolution video have an impact on the embedded watermark signal. Caenegem et al. [2] describe the design of a watermarking scheme resilient to H.264/SVC but treat the encoding only from a robustness point of view. In [19], Shi et al. propose a wavelet-domain embedding approach that exploits the transform's multi-resolution representation to cope with different resolution and quality layers. Both aforementioned techniques employ high-definition video frames (with HDTV and 4CIF resolution, respectively).

Finally, the third scenario appears to be overly complex from an implementation point of view given the intra-frame [6] and inter-layer prediction structure of H.264/SVC which necessitates drift compensation to minimize error propagation [11,4]. Zou et al. [24,23] propose a bitstream replacement watermark by altering H.264 CAVLC and CABAC symbols of HDTV video content several minutes long; scalability features are not addressed.

Integrated H.264/SVC video encoding and watermarking as shown in Fig. 4 offers control over the bitstream; for example the watermark can be placed exclusively in non-zero quantized residual coefficients [12]. Further, the embedding

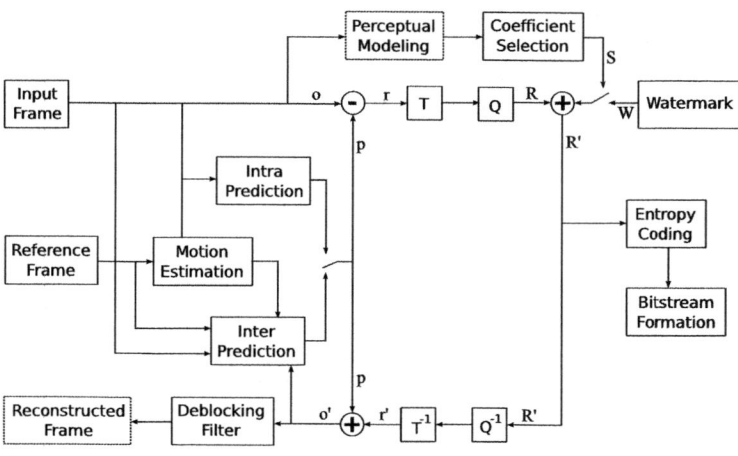

Fig. 2. Watermark embedding in quantized 4×4 DCT residual blocks

operation can efficiently be implemented in the same transform domain as used by the encoder. A combined encryption and watermarking-based authentication method for H.264/SVC encoding is proposed by Park and Shin [13]. Authentication information is encoded in the bits signalling the intra prediction mode, but can not be verified on the decoded video. Many proposals for H.264 integrated watermarking have been put forward using spread-spectrum or replacement techniques for authentication and copyright protection (e.g. [15,22,18,9]), however, watermarking of a scalable bitstream and the bitrate overhead is not considered. Recently, Park and Shin [14] put forward a method altering the DC coefficient of intra-coded blocks for copyright protection of H.264/SVC encoded content. The observed bit rate increase of over 10 % for certain sequences prompts for a more efficient solution.

The present work is an extension of [10]. A robust watermark is embedded in intra-coded frames during H.264/SVC encoding and detectable in the bitstream and decoded frames. In Section 2 we briefly review the H.264 watermarking framework [11] and investigate its applicability for protecting resolution-scalable video encoded with H.264/SVC. We propose a propagation step of the base-layer watermark signal in Section 3 in order to extend the framework to H.264/SVC, including resolution and quality scalability. Experimental results are provided in Section 4 followed by discussion and concluding remarks in Section 5.

2   Watermarking of H.264-Encoded Video

Several strategies have been proposed for embedding a watermark in H.264-encoded video. Most commonly, the watermark signal is placed in the quantized AC coefficients of intra-coded macroblocks. Noorkami et al. [11] present a framework where the Watson perceptual model for 8×8 DCT coefficients blocks [21] is adapted for the 4×4 integer approximation to the DCT which is predominantly used in H.264. Other embedding approaches include the modification of motion vectors or quantization of the DC term of each DCT block [3], however, the watermark can not be detected in the decoded video sequence or the scheme has to deal with prediction error drift.

2.1   Watermark Embedding

Figure 2 illustrates the structure of the watermarking framework integrated in the H.264 encoder; each macroblock of the input frame is coded using either intra- or inter-frame prediction and the difference between input pixels and prediction signal is the residual[1]. We denote by $r_{i,j,k}$ the coefficients of 4×4 spatial domain residual block k with $0 \leq i, j < 4$ and similarly by $o_{i,j,k}$ and $p_{i,j,k}$ the values of the original pixels and the prediction signal, respectively. Each block is transformed and quantized, T denotes the DCT and Q the quantization operation in the figure. Let $R_{i,j,k}$ represent the corresponding quantized DCT coefficients obtained by $R_k = \mathsf{Q}(\mathsf{T}(r_k))$. $R_{0,0,k}$ thus denotes the quantized DC coefficient of block k. After watermark embedding, described in the following paragraphs, and entropy coding, the residual information is written to the output bitstream.

For each block, a bipolar, pseudo-random watermark $W_{i,j,k} \in \{-1, 1\}$ with equiprobable symbols is generated and added to the residual block to construct the watermark block R',

$$R'_{i,j,k} = R_{i,j,k} + S_{i,j,k} \cdot W_{i,j,k}, \tag{1}$$

where $S_{i,j,k} \in \{0, 1\}$ selects the embedding locations for block k. The design of S determines the properties of the watermarking scheme and differentiates between various approaches: in [11], embedding locations are selected based on the masked error visibility thresholds derived from the Watson perceptual model. Further, the number of locations is constrained to avoid error pooling and AC coefficients of large magnitude are preferred in the selection process.

The pixels of the reconstructed, watermarked video frame are given by $o'_{i,j,k} = p_{i,j,k} + r'_{i,j,k}$ where

$$r'_k = \mathsf{T}^{-1}(\mathsf{Q}^{-1}(R'_k)) = \mathsf{T}^{-1}(\mathsf{Q}^{-1}(R_k) + Q_k \cdot S_k \cdot W_k). \tag{2}$$

For simplicity, we have dropped the coefficient indices i, j.

2.2   Blind Watermark Detection

Watermark detection is performed *blind*, i.e. without reference to the original host signal, and can be formulated as a hypothesis test to decide between

$$\begin{aligned} \mathcal{H}_0 &: Y_l = O_l \text{ (no/other watermark)} \\ \mathcal{H}_1 &: Y_l = O_l + Q_l \cdot W_l \text{ (watermarked)} \end{aligned} \tag{3}$$

---

[1] Other modes are possible, e.g. *PCM* or *skip* mode, but rarely occur or are not applicable for embedding an imperceptible watermark due to lack of texture.

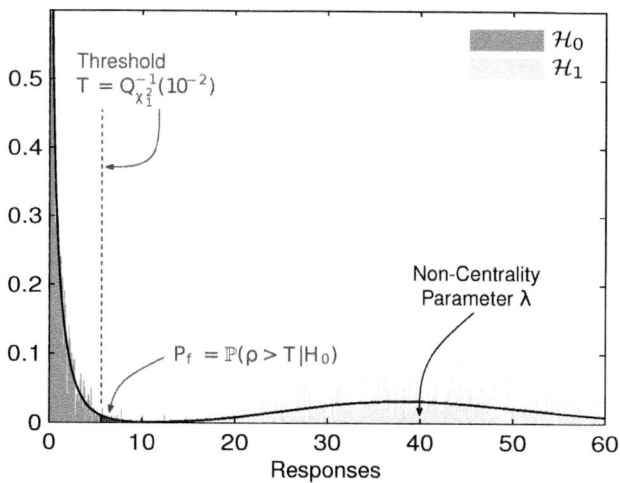

Fig. 3. Illustration of χ_1^2 detection response statistics under $\mathcal{H}_0$ and $\mathcal{H}_1$

where O_l denotes the selected 4×4 DCT coefficients of the received video frames, Q_l the corresponding quantization step size and W_l the elements of the watermark sequence; l indicates the lth selected coefficient or watermark bit to simplify notation. We adhere to the location-aware detection (LAD) scenario [12] where the embedding positions are known to the detector. For efficient blind watermark detection, accurate modeling of the host signal is required. We assume a Cauchy distribution of the DCT coefficients [1] and chose the Rao-Cauchy (RC) detector [7] whose detection statistic for the received signal Y_l of length L and the test against a detection threshold T are given by

$$\rho(Y_l) = \frac{8\hat{\gamma}^2}{L} \left[\sum_{l=1}^{L} \frac{Y_l \cdot W_l}{\hat{\gamma}^2 + Y_l^2} \right]^2 \quad \text{and} \quad \rho(Y_l) \gtrless_{\mathcal{H}_0}^{\mathcal{H}_1} T. \tag{4}$$

$\hat{\gamma}$ is an estimate of the Cauchy probability density function shape parameter which can be computed using fast, approximate methods [20]. According to [5], $\rho(Y_l)$ follows a Chi-Square distribution (χ_1^2) with one degree of freedom under $\mathcal{H}_0$ and we can write the probability of false-alarm $P_f = \mathbb{P}(\rho(Y_l) > T | \mathcal{H}_0)$ as

$$P_f = 2 Q\left(\sqrt{T}\right) \quad \text{and express} \quad T = \left[Q^{-1}\left(\frac{P_f}{2}\right) \right]^2 \tag{5}$$

where $Q(\cdot)$ denotes the Q-function of the Normal distribution (exploiting the relation $Q_{\chi_1^2}(x) = 2Q(\sqrt{x})$ with the Q-function of the χ_1^2 distribution). Note that no parameters need to be estimated to establish the detection threshold. The Rao-Cauchy test is a constant false-alarm rate detector [5] which simplifies the experimental setup. Under $\mathcal{H}_1$, the test statistic follows a non-central Chi-Square distribution $\chi_{1,\lambda}^2$ with one degree of freedom and non-centrality parameter λ.

By estimating λ from experimental detection responses, the performance of the detector can be analyzed in terms of the probability of missing the watermark,

$$P_m = 1 - \mathbb{P}(\rho > T | \mathcal{H}_1) = 1 - Q(\sqrt{T} - \sqrt{\lambda}) + Q(\sqrt{T} + \sqrt{\lambda}). \tag{6}$$

Figure 3 shows a histogram of the detection responses obtained by Eq. 4 under both hypothesis as well as the probability density functions of the χ_1^2 distributions which fit the observed data. The non-centrality parameter λ can be estimated from detector responses $\rho(Y_l)_p$, $1 \leq p \leq P$ obtained from P experiments

$$\hat{\lambda} = \left(\sum_{p=1}^{P} \sqrt{\rho(Y_l)_p} \right)^2 \tag{7}$$

and plugged into Eq. 6 to derive the *estimated* probability of missing the watermark. The measure obtained can be immediately interpreted and compared in a more meaningful way than – for example – a correlation coefficient or signal-to-noise ratio. However, some caution is in place with regard to the absolute value as usually only a small number of experiments (e.g. $P = 1000$) can be performed.

3   Extension to H.264/SVC

H.264/SVC resorts to several coding tools in order to predict enhancement layer data from the base layer representation [16] and exploit the statistical dependencies: (a) inter-layer intra prediction can adaptively use the (upsampled) reconstructed reference signal of intra-coded macroblocks, (b) macroblock partitioning and motion information of the base layer is carried over via inter-layer motion prediction for inter-coded macroblocks, and (c) inter-layer residual prediction allows to reduce the residual energy of inter-coded macroblocks in the enhancement layer by subtracting the (upsampled) transform domain residual coefficients of the colocated reference block. See Fig. 4 for an illustration.

In this work we focus on watermark embedding in intra-coded macroblocks of an H.264-coded base layer using the method reviewed in Section 2.

3.1   Resolution Scalability

In case a spatial enhancement layer with twice the resolution in each dimension is to be coded for SVC spatial scalability, the watermarked base-layer representation can be adaptively used for predicting the enhancement layer. In inter-layer intra prediction mode, the transform-domain enhancement layer residual of a 4×4 block k^E colocated with reference layer block k^B is given by

$$R_{k^E}'^E = Q(T(o_{k^E}^E - H \uparrow (o_{k^B}'^B))) \tag{8}$$

and the reconstructed, full-resolution video pixels are obtained by

$$o_{k^E}'^E = H \uparrow (o_{k^B}'^B) + T^{-1}(Q^{-1}(R_{k^E}'^E)). \tag{9}$$

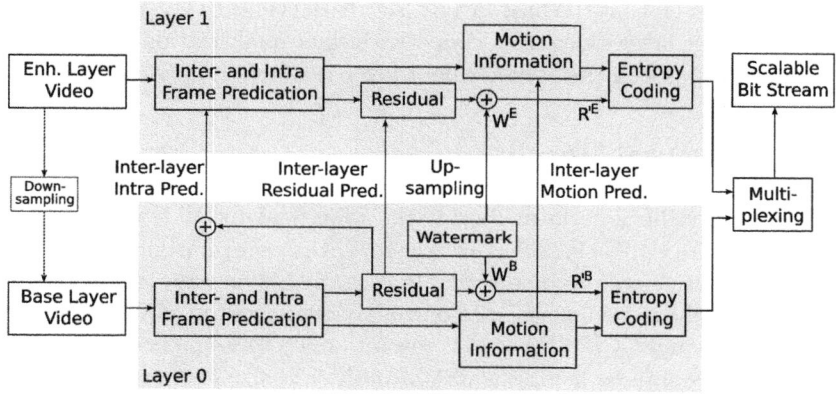

Fig. 4. Simplified H.264/SVC encoding and watermarking structure for two spatial resolution layers

H ↑ denotes the normative H.264/SVC upsampling operation and superscripts ^{B} and ^{E} indicate base and spatial enhancement layer data, respectively. Apparently, the first right-hand term of Eq. (9) represents the upsampled, watermarked base-layer signal and the second term the quantized difference to the full-resolution, original video. Depending on the quantization parameter used to code the enhancement layer, the base-layer watermark can propagate to the decoded enhancement-layer video. Coarse quantization preserves a stronger watermark signal as illustrated in Figure 5 (a).

Watermarking only the base layer data is clearly not effective in protecting the full-resolution video. Not only does the watermark fade away, but also the bit rate for the enhancement layer increases, see Table 3, due to the added independent watermark signal which increased energy of the residual $R'^E_{k^E}$. To remedy these shortcomings, we propose to upsample the base layer watermark signal

$$W^E_{k^E} = \mathsf{Q}(\mathsf{T}(\mathsf{H}\uparrow(\mathsf{T}^{-1}(Q_{k^B}\cdot S_{k^B}\cdot W^B_{k^B})))) \tag{10}$$

and add the resulting enhancement layer watermark $W^E_{k^E}$ to the residual blocks $R'^E_{k^E}$ to form *compensated* residual blocks

$$R''^E_{k^E} = R'^E_{k^E} + W^E_{k^E}. \tag{11}$$

Watermark detection is always performed with the base-layer watermark W, the full-resolution video is downsampled for detection.

3.2 Quality Scalability

In Fig. 5 (b) we plot the watermark transfer between two QCIF coarse-grain scalability (CGS) quality layers for a range of coding quantization parameters. The quality enhancement layer is coded using $QP-3$ with respect to the base layer. It can be seen that the base layer watermark is effectively overshadowed by the enhancement layer video data coded with finer quantization. Simply adding the same watermark in the enhancement layer restores the watermark signal.

4   Experimental Results

Experiments have been performed using the Joint Scalable Video Model (JSVM) reference software version 9.19.9. Source code for the watermarking schemes investigated in this article will become available at http://www.wavelab.at/sources. All experiments have been performed on widely-available test video sequences[2] in CIF (352×288) and QCIF (176×144) resolution; QCIF sequences have been obtained by downsampling using the JSVM tools. Experiments are repeated 1000 times with different watermark seeds to estimate the detection performance.

The watermark is embedded in the base layer as described in Section 2 with an average target PSNR in the luminance channel of 40 dB between the original and the coded and watermarked video. We opt for always selecting the first 4×4 DCT AC coefficient in zig-zag order as the embedding location when it is non-zero; formally

$$S_{i,j,k} = \begin{cases} 1 & i = 0, j = 1 \wedge R_{0,1,k} \neq 0 \\ 0 & \text{otherwise} \end{cases} \quad \forall k.$$

The upsampled watermark signal is added to the quantized, transform-domain enhancement layer residuals as proposed in Section 3.1 with a target PSNR of 40 dB. The resulting watermarked, resolution-scalable bitstream can be decoded into QCIF and CIF video sequences.

For video quality scalability (cf. Section 3.2), the base-layer watermark is propagated to the enhancement layer and the coarse-grain quality scalable bitstream can be decoded into two differently quantized representations.

We first address watermark detection on the decoded video frames. Then watermark detection directly on the residual transform coefficients after arithmetic decoding is considered, e.g. for copy control or authentication applications.

4.1   Watermark Detection on the Decoded Video Frames

Figure 5 shows the watermark detection performance for the *Foreman* sequence in terms of probability of miss (P_m) as a function of the H.264/SVC quantization parameter QP varying from 20 to 35. In the experiment, the false-alarm rate (P_f) is set to 10^{-3} and detection is performed on the first frame only; base layer and spatial resolution enhancement layer have been coded with the same QP (cf. Fig. 5a), the coarse grain quality enhancement layer (cf. Fig. 5b) with $QP - 3$ relative to the base layer. The watermark can be reliably detected in the decoded base layer video (L0). Detection performance increases with coarser quantization

---

[2] The uncoded test sequences are available for download from
http://media.xiph.org/video/derf/.

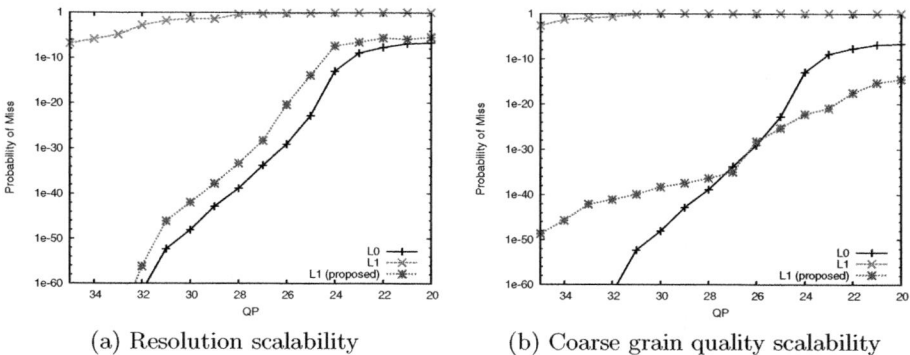

(a) Resolution scalability   (b) Coarse grain quality scalability

Fig. 5. Transfer of the base-layer watermark to a (a) spatial resolution, and (b) coarse-gain quality enhancement layer for different quantization parameters (QP)

as the watermark signal gets stronger relative to the host – remember that we added ± 1 to the quantized residual.

We observe that the watermark embedded in the base layer is hardly detectable in the enhancement layer (L1). Only for coarse quantization ($QP \geq 28$) when no residual information is coded for most L1 blocks and solely the interlayer intra prediction signal is available for reconstruction, detection becomes possible. However, using the upsampled base layer watermark, watermark detection performance in the enhancement layer is substantially improved (*L1 proposed*) and mostly restored to the level of the base layer watermark.

Table 1 provides the watermark detection results for six resolution-scalable H.264/SVC video sequences coded with $QP = 25$. The second column (*L0*) shows the probability of missing the watermark (P_m) for the decoded video in base layer QCIF resolution. When the watermark is embedded just in the base layer (column *L1 BL WM*), the watermark is not detectable using the decoded enhancement layer CIF resolution video since the base layer watermark does not propagate to the higher resolution layer. The fourth column (*L1 indep. WM*) lists the detection results for an independent watermark embedded in the enhancement layer. As the host signal is now four times larger, the probability of miss is drastically reduced. When the upsampled watermark signal is added to the enhancement layer residual (column *L1 proposed*) as presented in Section 3, the watermark can be reliably detected from the decoded CIF video sequence.

4.2   Watermark Detection on the Partially Decoded Bitstream

Table 2 shows the watermark detection results directly on the residual transform coefficients after arithmetic decoding of the bitstream, i.e. detection integrated in the H.264/SVC decoder. The encoder settings are the same as above.

First, we observe than detection performance is higher when operating on the residual coefficients compared to detection on the decoded video frames (cf.

Table 1. Detection results on the decoded base (L0) and resolution enhancement layer (L1) video frames

Sequence	Probability of Miss ($P_f = 10^{-3}$)			
	L0	L1 (BL WM)	L1 (indep. WM)	L1 (proposed)
Foreman	$2.3 \cdot 10^{-25}$	0.81	~ 0.0	$3.2 \cdot 10^{-17}$
Soccer	$2.6 \cdot 10^{-69}$	1.0	~ 0.0	$1.1 \cdot 10^{-49}$
Bus	$1.0 \cdot 10^{-8}$	1.0	$2.5 \cdot 10^{-316}$	$6.2 \cdot 10^{-8}$
Container	$5.2 \cdot 10^{-119}$	0.44	~ 0.0	$1.1 \cdot 10^{-91}$
Coastguard	$9.8 \cdot 10^{-133}$	0.68	~ 0.0	$5.2 \cdot 10^{-97}$
Stefan	$8.5 \cdot 10^{-30}$	0.91	~ 0.0	$3.2 \cdot 10^{-23}$

Tables 1 and 2, column *L0*). This is expected as H.264 spatial prediction acts as an additional additive noise source on the residual signal where the watermark is embedded.

Second, the base layer watermark can be reliably detected in the partially decoded enhancement layer bitstream (column *L1 BL WM*). For watermark detection, the enhancement layer residual blocks $R_{k^E}^E$ are downsampled

$$R_{k^B}^{\prime B} = \mathsf{Q}(\mathsf{T}(\mathsf{H} \downarrow (\mathsf{T}^{-1}(\mathsf{Q}^{-1}(R_{k^E}^E))))) \tag{12}$$

so that the base layer watermark W_k can be correlated with the colocated blocks $R_{k^B}^{\prime B}$ of base layer resolution.

Note that the $R_{k^B}^{\prime B}$ actually contain the inverted watermark $-W$ when H.264/SVC inter-layer intra prediction is used since

$$r_{k^E}^E = o_{k^E}^E - \mathsf{H} \uparrow (o_{k^B}^{\prime B}) \tag{13}$$

where $o_{k^B}^{\prime B}$ contains the additive base layer watermark W. However, the Rao-Cauchy detector employed is agnostic to the sign of the watermark due to the square operation in Eq. 4.

The use of inter-layer intra prediction for enhancement layer coding can be an adaptive decision of the H.264/SVC encoder. For the experiments, the adaptive decision was enabled in the JSVM reference implementation and it is observed that the majority of intra-coded blocks are in fact coded with inter-layer prediction.

4.3   Bit Rate Assessment of Watermarked Scalability Layers

In Table 3 we examine the bit rate (in Kbit/s) of the resolution-scalable bitstream for the first 32 frames of six test sequences coded with $QP = 25$ and inter-layer prediction. Results have been averaged over 10 test runs with different watermarks. For reference, the second column (*L1 no WM*) lists the bit rates

Table 2. Detection results on partially decoded base (L0) and resolution enhancement layer (L1) coefficients

Sequence	Probability of Miss ($P_f = 10^{-3}$)	
	L0	L1 (BL WM)
Foreman	$3.8 \cdot 10^{-48}$	$1.6 \cdot 10^{-44}$
Soccer	$1.1 \cdot 10^{-107}$	$1.5 \cdot 10^{-84}$
Bus	$5.4 \cdot 10^{-35}$	$1.1 \cdot 10^{-32}$
Container	$4.7 \cdot 10^{-198}$	$8.0 \cdot 10^{-95}$
Coastguard	$2.2 \cdot 10^{-210}$	$2.4 \cdot 10^{-88}$
Stefan	$8.1 \cdot 10^{-77}$	$1.7 \cdot 10^{-41}$

for coding the sequences without any watermark. The third column (*L1 BL WM*) contains the bit rate when watermarking the base layer only. We notice an increase of about 3% on average due to the added watermark signal. The fourth column (*L1 indep. WM*) lists the bit rate when independent watermarks are added to the base and enhancement layer; two independent watermarks in the two layer produces the highest bitrate. The rightmost column (*L1 proposed*) presents the results when adding the upsampled watermark to the enhancement layer residual as proposed. Surprisingly, the bit rate can be reduced compared to the previous two columns and is lower than having no watermark in the decoded enhancement layer at all.

The reason follows from the observations made in Section 4.2: in case inter-layer intra prediction is employed by the H.264/SVC encoder, the enhancement layer bitstream codes the difference between the upsampled base layer recon-struction (the prediction) and the full-resolution video signal. An additional, uncorrelated watermark signal increases that difference and hence the enhance-ment layer bitrate as shown in column *L1 BL WM*. When the upsampled wa-termark is added to the enhancement layer video, the prediction (containing the base layer watermark) better matches the enhancement layer data to be coded and hence reduces the bitrate.

Table 4 lists the bit rates in Kbit/s for the coarse-grain quality (CGS) enhance-ment layer. The QCIF base layer is coded with $QP = 30$ and the enhancement layer of the same resolution with $QP = 24$. We can observe that watermarking the enhancement layer with the same watermark as the base layer (column *L1 proposed*) slightly reduces the bit rate over the case where the enhancement does not carry a watermark (column *L1 BL WM*) and only the base layer (BL) is watermarked, or – to a larger extent – when a different watermark (column *L1 indep. WM*) is embedded in the two quality scalability layers.

H.264/SVC also supports so-called medium-grain scalability (MGS) to enable quality adaptation without the need to code separate layers. MGS is realized by grouping the DCT coefficients in zig-zag order and allowing to discard the endmost coefficient groups. Since the watermark in this work is embedded in

Table 3. Bit rate of the resolution enhancement layer (L1)

Sequence	Bit rate (Kbit/s)			
	L1 (no WM)	L1 (BL WM)	L1 (indep. WM)	L1 (proposed)
Foreman	883.1	939.5	1018.9	924.5
Soccer	1188.0	1239.1	1303.8	1227.0
Bus	1693.0	1732.0	1779.0	1721.0
Container	906.6	957.7	982.1	944.7
Coastguard	1506.6	1557.8	1572.6	1534.2
Stefan	1621.4	1657.0	1715.0	1651.0

Table 4. Bit rate of the coarse-grain quality layer (L1)

Sequence	Bit rate (Kbit/s)			
	L1 (no WM)	L1 (BL WM)	L1 (indep. WM)	L1 (proposed)
Foreman	287.4	330.9	342.9	320.2
Soccer	342.7	380.6	401.3	371.6
Bus	463.8	500.0	507.4	490.5
Container	258.6	307.8	315.8	298.2
Coastguard	359.5	396.0	404.8	387.0
Stefan	483.1	525.8	536.0	517.5

the first AC coefficient, MGS does not impair the watermark detection results unless all AC coefficients are discarded.

5   Discussion and Conclusion

In this work, we considered the application of a robust H.264-integrated watermarking method [11] in the context of H.264/SVC. A watermark embedded in the base layer data of a resolution-scalable bitstream is not detectable in the full-resolution decoded video sequence. We can resolve the issue by adding a compensation watermark signal to the enhancement layer residual which also reduces teh bitrate. The base layer watermark can be detected in the decoded video frames *and* the compressed domain, i.e. after entropy decoding of the residual data. With respect to the enhancement layer, the base layer watermark can be either detected in the compressed domain residual data, *or* the decoded video frames due to inter-layer prediction of H.264/SVC when employing the proposed compensation technique. Li et al. [8] discuss watermarking of a scalable audio bitstream and focus on the first case.

We provide detection results for base- and enhancement layer watermarking and consider the bitrate of the resulting watermarked scalable bitstream. Contrary to other recent approaches [19,2] we focus on the particularities of watermarking integrated in the H.264/SVC encoding step as opposed to watermarking before scalable bitstream formation.

The 8×8 DCT which is more efficient for coding high-resolution frames can be permitted for coding the enhancement layer, only the base layer watermark is constrained to embedding in the prevalent 4×4 transform blocks since the watermark detector is blind and has no information on the H.264/SVC mode decisions. Upsampling the watermark cannot be easily extended to support several resolution enhancement layers as the watermark signal looses its high-pass characteristic; on the other hand, multi-layer H.264/SVC bitstreams have increasingly higher bit rate compared to non-scalable coding and are not likely to be adopted.

Further work includes an assessment of different embedding strategies (incorporating perceptual shaping of the watermark) with regard to the bitrate of the watermarked bitstream and a comparison of blind detection approaches adapted to the quantized host signal coefficients.

References

1. Altunbasak, Y., Kamaci, N.: An analysis of the DCT coefficient distribution with the H.264 video coder. In: Proceedings of the IEEE International Conference on Acoustics, Speech and Signal Processing, ICASSP 2004, vol. 3, pp. 177–180. IEEE, Montreal (2004)
2. van Caenegem, R., Dooms, A., Barbarien, J., Schelkens, P.: Design of an H.264/SVC resilient watermarking scheme. In: Proceedings of SPIE, Multimedia on Mobile Devices 2010, vol. 7542. SPIE, San Jose (2010)
3. Gong, X., Lu, H.M.: Towards fast and robust watermarking scheme for H.264 video. In: Proceedings of the IEEE International Symposium on Multimedia, ISM 2008, pp. 649–653. IEEE, Berkeley (2008)
4. Hartung, F., Girod, B.: Watermarking of uncompressed and compressed video. Signal Processing 66(3), 283–301 (1998)
5. Kay, S.M.: Fundamentals of Statistical Signal Processing: Detection Theory, vol. 2. Prentice-Hall (1998)
6. Kim, D.W., Choi, Y.G., Kim, H.S., Yoo, J.S., Choi, H.J., Seo, Y.H.: The problems in digital watermarking into intra-frames of H.264/AVC. Image and Vision Computing 28(8), 1220–1228 (2010)
7. Kwitt, R., Meerwald, P., Uhl, A.: A lightweight Rao-Cauchy detector for additive watermarking in the DWT-domain. In: Proceedings of the ACM Multimedia and Security Workshop (MMSEC 2008), pp. 33–41. ACM, Oxford (2008)
8. Li, Z., Sun, Q., Lian, Y.: Design and analysis of a scalable watermarking scheme for the scalable audio coder. IEEE Transactions on Signal Processing 54(8), 3064–3077 (2006)
9. Lin, S., Chuang, C.Y., Meng, H.C.: A video watermarking in H.265/AVC encoder. In: Proceedings of the 5th International Conference on Intelligent Information Hiding and Multimedia Signal Processing, IIH-MSP 2009, Kyoto, Japan, pp. 340–343 (September 2009)

10. Meerwald, P., Uhl, A.: Robust Watermarking of H.264/SVC-Encoded Video: Quality and Resolution Scalability. In: Kim, H.-J., Shi, Y.Q., Barni, M. (eds.) IWDW 2010. LNCS, vol. 6526, pp. 159–169. Springer, Heidelberg (2011)

11. Noorkami, M., Mersereau, R.M.: A framework for robust watermarking of H.264 encoded video with controllable detection performance. IEEE Transactions on Information Forensics and Security 2(1), 14–23 (2007)

12. Noorkami, M., Mersereau, R.M.: Digital video watermarking in P-frames with controlled video bit-rate increase. IEEE Transactions on Information Forensics and Security 3(3), 441–455 (2008)

13. Park, S.W., Shin, S.U.: Combined Scheme of Encryption and Watermarking in H.264/Scalable Video Coding (SVC). In: Tsihrintzis, G.A., et al. (eds.) New Direct. in Intel. Interac. Multimedia. SCI, vol. 142, pp. 351–361. Springer, Heidelberg (2008)

14. Park, S.W., Shin, S.U.: Authentication and copyright protection scheme for H.264/AVC and SVC. Journal of Information Science and Engineering 27, 129–142 (2011)

15. Qiu, G., Marziliano, P., Ho, A.T.S., He, D., Sun, Q.: A hybrid watermarking scheme for H.264/AVC video. In: Proceedings of the 17th International Conference on Pattern Recognition, ICPR 2004, pp. 865–868. IEEE, Cambridge (2004)

16. Schwarz, H., Wien, M.: The scalable video coding extension of the H.264/AVC standard. IEEE Signal Processing Magazine 25(2), 135–141 (2008)

17. Segall, C.A., Sullivan, G.J.: Spatial scalability within the H.264/AVC scalable video coding extension. IEEE Transactions on Circuits and Systems for Video Technology 17(9), 1121–1135 (2007)

18. Shahid, Z., Meuel, P., Chaumont, M., Puech, W.: Considering the reconstruction loop for watermarking of intra and inter frames of H.264/AVC. In: Proceedings of the 17th European Signal Processing Conference, EUSIPCO 2009, pp. 1794–1798. EURASIP, Glasgow (2009)

19. Shi, F., Liu, S., Yao, H., Liu, Y., Zhang, S.: Scalable and Credible Video Watermarking Towards Scalable Video Coding. In: Qiu, G., Lam, K.M., Kiya, H., Xue, X.-Y., Kuo, C.-C.J., Lew, M.S. (eds.) PCM 2010, Part I. LNCS, vol. 6297, pp. 697–708. Springer, Heidelberg (2010)

20. Tsihrintzis, G., Nikias, C.: Fast estimation of the parameters of alpha–stable impulsive interference. IEEE Transactions on Signal Processing 44(6), 1492–1503 (1996)

21. Watson, A.B.: DCT quantization matrices visually optimized for individual images. In: Proceedings of SPIE, International Conference on Human Vision, Visual Processing and Display, pp. 202–216. SPIE, San Jose (1993)

22. Zhang, J., Ho, A.T.S., Qiu, G., Marziliano, P.: Robust video watermarking of H.264/AVC. IEEE Transactions on Circuits and Systems 54(2), 205–209 (2007)

23. Zou, D., Bloom, J.: H.264 stream replacement watermarking with CABAC encoding. In: Proceedings of the IEEE International Conference on Multimedia and Expo, ICME 2010, Singapore (July 2010)

24. Zou, D., Bloom, J.: H.264/AVC substitution watermarking: a CAVLC example. In: Proceedings of the SPIE, Media Forensics and Security, vol. 7254. SPIE, San Jose (2009)

PC-Based Real-Time Video Watermark Embedding System Independent of Platform for Parallel Computing

Takaaki Yamada[1], Isao Echizen[2], and Hiroshi Yoshiura[3]

[1] Yokohama Research Laboratory, Hitachi, Ltd., Totsuka-ku, Yokohama, Japan
[2] National Institute of Informatics, Chiyoda-ku, Tokyo, Japan
[3] The University of Electro-Communications, Electro-Communication, Chofu, Tokyo, Japan
takaaki.yamada.tr@hitachi.com, iechizen@nii.ac.jp,
yoshiura@hc.uec.ac.jp

Abstract. An improved system is described for embedding watermarks into video frames in real time using software running on an ordinary personal computer and that is independent of the parallel-computing platform. It uses standard video I/O and is separate from the encoding process, so it can be incorporated into various types of encoding and distribution systems, which makes it well suited for distributing live content. Real-time processing is achieved by making the watermark-pattern generation process common to every frame a pre-process and by reusing the watermark pattern output from this pre-process. It is also achieved by storing the watermarked video frames into video memory on the video I/O board, thereby eliminating the need for storing them in buffers on hard disk. Testing of a prototype system for standard-definition video demonstrated the validity of this approach.

Keywords: video watermark, real-time processing, shortening processing time, software application system, content security.

1 Introduction

Digital content—such as pictures, videos, and music—is being made widely available because of its advantages over analog content. It requires less space, is easier to process, and is not degraded by aging or repeated use. The wide use of broadband networks and high-efficiency personal computers (PCs) enables live digital video content, such as concerts and distance education, to be distributed over the Internet. A serious problem, however, is that the copyright of digital content is easily violated because the content can be easily copied and redistributed through the Internet. Digital watermarking, which helps protect the copyright of digital content by embedding copyright information into it, is one countermeasure for content security [1, 2]. Video watermark (WM) embedding in real time is an essential requirement for live content distribution.

Systems have been developed for real-time processing that use dedicated hardware [3–5] or a specific parallel-computing platform [6, 7]. Real-time WM embedding using multiprocessing is well-suited to applications in which video content must be

Y.Q. Shi (Ed.): Transactions on DHMS VII, LNCS 7110, pp. 15–33, 2012.

distributed with high efficiency, such as broadcasting. However, dedicated hardware may cause cost problems in terms of installation and maintenance and in version upgrading. Moreover, the parallel-computing platform specified may not be installed in the customer's PCs.

To overcome these problems, we previously developed a real-time WM embedding system suitable for content distribution that uses software running on an ordinary PC [8]. This software-based system enables real-time processing including WM embedding, MPEG encoding, and hard disk drive (HDD) recording. However, it can generate only MPEG-4 encoded WMed files because the WM embedding process is combined with the MPEG-4 encoding process. Moreover, it supports only the QVGA (320×240-pixel) format, which is converted from the VGA (640×480-pixel) format of the incoming video signal, to reduce the total processing time.

We have modified this system so that it is directly handle the VGA format of the incoming video signal [9, 10], and so that it is independent of the parallel-computing platform. We also separate it from the encoding process so that it can be incorporated in various types of encoding and distributing systems.

Section 2 overviews video watermarking and describes previous real-time WM embedding systems. Section 3 introduces our improved real-time WM embedding system and describes our prototype system. Section 4 presents the results of our experimental evaluation. Section 5 presents an alternate system implementation based on a different watermarking algorithm to highlight the effectiveness of the proposed platform-independent approach. Section 6 concludes with a summary of the key points.

2   Video Watermarking

2.1   Assumed Use

We assume that digital watermarking is used to embed identifier (ID) information in videos, helping to protect video content distributed over networks from content servers to client PCs. As illustrated in Figure 1, watermarks (WMs) representing ID information are embedded into video images that are then compressed using an encoder such as an MPEG encoder. The video provider then distributes the images over a network. When the WMed images are received, they are decoded, enabling the user to view them on a PC. If the user copies and redistributes the images (for example, by placing them on a web page), an auditor can detect the embedded ID information and notify the provider of the copying. The video provider could then even identify the copier if the images contained embedded information identifying the user to whom they had been provided.

The copier may convert the file format of watermarked video into another one to reduce the size of video data. However, when PCs and networks have enough resources for the user to playback and redistribute video images over networks, the user does not need to modify the video images. To simplify the discussion and focus on system performance for real-time processing, we assume that the video images are not transcoded, i.e. WMs are not attacked by the user.

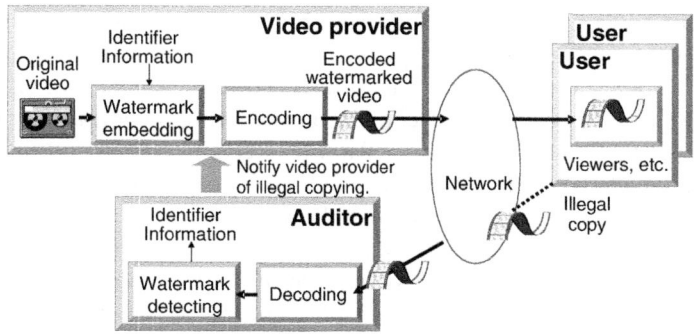

Fig. 1. Assumed use of video watermark embedding

2.2   Technical Requirements

Video WMs should not noticeably degrade image quality; i.e., they should not interfere with the user's perception. Nonetheless, they should be robust enough to be reliably detected after common video processing such as MPEG encoding. Because real-time content such as concerts and distance education is becoming widely available through distribution over networks, real-time WM embedding is an essential requirement.

2.3   Conventional Real-Time Systems

Several systems for embedding WMs into video content in real-time have been developed and tested. They use dedicated hardware such as a field programmable gate array (FPGA) [4] or media processors [5]. Terada et al. developed a hardware-based system using media processors that is intended for real-time WM embedding for high-definition TV (HDTV 1080i). Parallel processing is done using very-long-instruction-word (VLIW)-based media processors [5]. This system is suitable for broadcasting of media because the hardware enables high-efficiency processing. However, hardware embedding could cause cost problems in terms of installation and maintenance, and version upgrading could be difficult.

Parallelized software running on a specific PC-platform enables real-time watermarking [6, 7]. Real-time WM detection in standard-definition TV (SDTV) content is achieved by using multithreading on a PC [6]. Real-time WM embedding in HDTV content is achieved by using SIMD (single instruction, multiple data) operations on a PC [7]. These software implementation techniques can speed up throughput times when a specific parallel-computing platform is used. However, they do not work well when another parallel-computing platform is used. Moreover, platform-specific software implementations may have compatibility problems in various customer environments from the software product viewpoint.

PCs commonly support parallel computing in hardware, such as by disk caching. They also use parallel computing techniques in the operation system, such as for process management. Although parallel-computing platform are often used for running software applications, applications should be independent of not only the commonly-used parallel-computing platforms, but also the system-specific one, as much as possible. If the processing time was reduced by using a speedup method in the application-software layer, the combination of the speedup method and proven methods using parallel-computing platforms could potentially improve the performance much more than using each method alone. We previously reported such software techniques that are independent of the parallel-computing platform [8, 9].

An overview of the real-time WM embedding system we previously developed is shown in Figure 2 [8]. The previous system runs on a PC with a video-capture board and provides real-time encoding by software processing on the PC. The system receives NTSC (National Television System Committee) video signal output from a video camera or other video source. The incoming signal is converted into QVGA format by the driver software on the video-capture board. As the video is encoded, the WM embedding process embeds WMs representing copyright information into each frame of the video. The WMed frames are then MPEG-4 encoded, and the WMed MPEG-4 bit stream is recorded on the hard disk. The embedding, MPEG-4 encoding, and HDD recording are all done in real time.

However, use of this system for live content distribution is problematic: (1) it generates only MPEG-4 encoded WMed files because the WM embedding process is combined with the MPEG-4 encoding process, (2) it can handle only QVGA format, which is converted from the VGA format of the incoming video signal, to reduce the total processing time, and (3) the encoded WMed stream files are stored only on the hard disk (there is no video interface with the distribution servers).

Our improved system overcomes these limitations. It is separate from the encoding process and is equipped with a standard video interface, so it can be used with various types of encoders and distribution servers. Moreover, it can directly handle the VGA format of the incoming video signal.

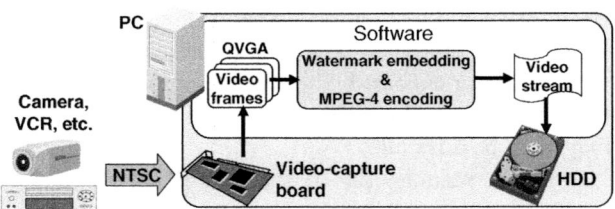

Fig. 2. System overview of previous real-time watermark embedding system

3   Improved System

3.1   Description

Our improved real-time video watermark (WM) embedding system is practical for live content distribution. It can be applied to various content distribution systems because it is equipped with a standard video interface (such as SDTV video I/O) and because it separates the encoding process from the WM embedding process. We achieved real-time processing for SDTV by dividing the WM embedding process into a pre-process common to every video frame and post-processes specific to each frame and by reducing the amount of calculation needed for WM embedding by reusing the data output from the pre-process for the post-processes. Moreover, because it runs on the user's existing PC, installation and upgrading are facilitated. The proposed system can also work with other functions on the PC, if there are sufficient computing resources.

As shown in Figure 3, the system runs on a PC with a video input and output (I/O) board and provides real-time WM embedding by software processing on the PC. The real-time encoding process receives a video signal output from a video camera, VCR, video player, or other video source. The incoming video frames in VGA (640×480-pixel) format are captured from the incoming signal and loaded into the video memory by the video I/O board driver software. The WM embedding process embeds WMs representing ID information into each frame of the video. The WMed frames are then uploaded into the video memory on the video I/O board. The WMed video contents are output, for instance, to an encoder and server, which then provide the content to clients, which have a viewer as shown in Figure 1.

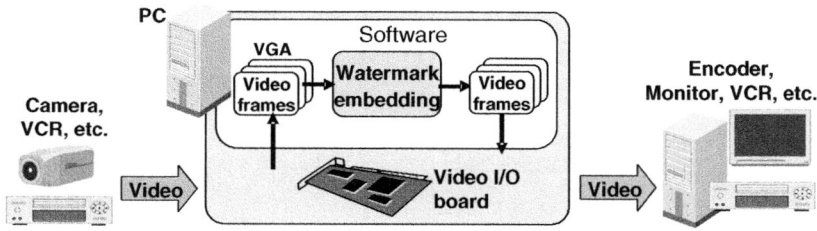

Fig. 3. System overview of improved real-time watermark embedding system

3.2   Improved Process Flow

Figure 4 illustrates the architecture of our improved software processing, from video input through output. The video input is an incoming signal, such as an NTSC signal, carrying a time sequence of video frames. The video frames are continuously transformed into an uncompressed format (such as YUV) one after another in the video memory on the video I/O board. The frame data are captured in real time and kept in internal memory until they are overwritten by the data in the next incoming frame. The previous system could handle only QVGA (320×240-pixel) format, converted from the VGA (640×480-pixel) format of the incoming video signal as shown in Figure 3. To enable the VGA format to be handled in real time, we

– divided the WM embedding process into a pre-process (WM pattern generation) common to every video frame and post-processes (WM strength calculation and WMed frame generation) specific to each frame,
– redesigned the data flow so that the post-processes could reuse the WM pattern output by the pre-process, and

- redesigned the frame flow so that the video frames are saved directly into the video memory on the video I/O board rather than in buffers on the hard disk.

The video output is an outgoing video signal, such as an NTSC signal, carrying a time sequence of watermarked video frames. If a video frame is not ready to be output, the previous frame in the video memory is reused instead. That is, a frame is dropped. To avoiding frame dropping, the frame data should be synchronously transformed into video output form in real time.

Various WM embedding processes have been proposed [11–14, 16–17]. We developed our real-time WM embedding process on the basis of a basic WM algorithm [11]. The process flow of the WM embedding is as follows. To simplify the description, we describe a 1-bit-WM schema. In the multiple-bit schema, each frame is divided into regions, and the 1-bit process is applied to each region.

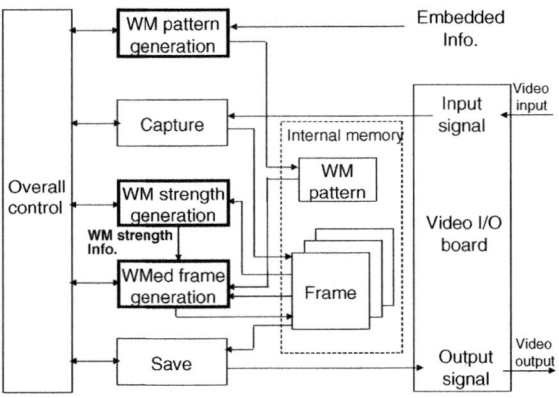

Fig. 4. System architecture of improved real-time WM embedding system

[WM embedding]
The luminance set of the f -th frame consisting of N pixels is $\mathbf{y}^{(f)} = \left\{ y_i^{(f)} \mid 1 \le i \le N \right\}$. The process flow of the 1-bit-WM embedding comprises six steps. The original luminance data $\mathbf{y}^{(f)}$ and the embedded information b are input parameters for the WM embedding process. The number of pixels N is a constant value. Pseudo random array $\tilde{\mathbf{m}}$ is calculated on the basis of this constant value. The watermarked luminance data $\mathbf{y}'^{(f)}$ is an output parameter.

Step 1: (pre-process, WM pattern generation): Generate WM pattern $\mathbf{m} = \left\{ m_i \mid 1 \le i \le N \right\}$ on the basis of the bit value of the embedded information b ;

$$\mathbf{m} = \begin{cases} \tilde{\mathbf{m}} & \text{if } b = 1 \\ -\tilde{\mathbf{m}} & \text{if } b = 0, \end{cases} \tag{1}$$

where $\tilde{\mathbf{m}}$ represents the set comprising a pseudo random array of N elements with a value of ± 1; that is, $\tilde{\mathbf{m}} = \left\{ \tilde{m}_i \in \{-1,+1\} \mid 1 \le i \le N \right\}$.

The generated WM pattern is then stored in internal memory.

Step 2: Do the following steps over $f = 1, 2, \ldots$.

Step 3: Store the input signal into the video memory on the video I/O board; generate original frame $\mathbf{y}^{(f)}$ from the captured signal, and store it in the internal memory.

Step 4: (post-process, WM strength calculation): Calculate the set of the WM strengths $\mathbf{s}^{(f)} = \left\{ s_i^{(f)} > 0 \mid 1 \le i \le N \right\}$ from the original frame, $\mathbf{y}^{(f)}$. Note that each strength $s_i^{(f)}$ represents WM imperceptibility at pixel i of the f-th frame. For instance, $s_i^{(f)}$ is the difference between the luminance value for the i-th pixel $y_i^{(f)}$ and the average luminance value for the surrounding eight pixels. Setting the WM strength in this way maintains the image quality by avoiding the embedding of a strong WM in a plain region (where the spatial frequency of the pixel values is low) in each frame.

Step 5: (post-process, WMed frame generation): Generate watermarked frame $\mathbf{y}'^{(f)} = \left\{ y_i'^{(f)} \mid 1 \le i \le N \right\}$ by adding the WM pattern m_i (obtained in Step 1) multiplied by the WM strength:

$$y_i'^{(f)} = y_i^{(f)} + s_i^{(f)} m_i . \tag{2}$$

Watermarked frame $\mathbf{y}'^{(f)}$ is then stored in the internal memory. Note that this process loads the WM pattern calculated in the pre-process; i.e., the data is reused.

Step 6: Convert watermarked frame $\mathbf{y}'^{(f)}$ into a video signal and save the signal into the video memory on the video board.

An example process flow of the corresponding WM detection comprises four steps.

[WM detection]
The same WMs are embedded in consecutive frames although the frame contents may change (e.g., the frames show a person moving). Therefore, if these frames are accumulated or superimposed on each other to form an average image, their watermark signals will accumulate while their content will almost disappear. We thus accumulate n consecutive frames to generate an average image from which the watermark is detected. The luminance set of the f'-th WMed frame consisting of N pixels is $\mathbf{y}'^{(f')} = \left\{ y_i'^{(f')} \mid 1 \le i \le N \right\}$ $(f' = 1, \ldots, n)$. The input parameters for the WM detection process are the WMed frames $\mathbf{y}'^{(f')}$ and the number of

accumulated frames n. The number of consisting pixels N and pseudo random array $\tilde{\mathbf{m}}$ have the same values as used in the WM embedding process.

Step 1: Do the following steps over n WMed frames $\mathbf{y}'^{(f')}$ $(f' = 1,...,n)$.

Step 2: Accumulate the n frames in $\tilde{\mathbf{y}} = \{\tilde{y}_i \mid 1 \leq i \leq N\}$. $\tilde{y}_i = 1/n \sum_{f=1}^{n} y_i'^{(f')}$.

Step 3: Calculate correlation value c by correlating pseudo random array $\tilde{\mathbf{m}}$ with accumulated frame $\tilde{\mathbf{y}}$. That is,

$$c = \frac{1}{N}\sum_i \tilde{m}_i \tilde{y}_i = \frac{1}{N}\sum_i \tilde{m}_i \left(\frac{1}{n}\sum_{f'=1}^{n} y_i'^{(f')}\right)$$
$$= \frac{1}{N}\sum_i \tilde{m}_i \left(\frac{1}{n}\sum_{f'=1}^{n} \left(y_i^{(f')} + s_i^{(f')} m_i\right)\right) = \frac{1}{nN}\left(\sum_{i,f'} \tilde{m}_i y_i^{(f')} \pm \sum_{i,f'} s_i^{(f')}\right). \tag{3}$$

Note that the first term, $\sum_{i,f'} \tilde{m}_i y_i^{(f')}$, is expected to be near to zero due to the randomness of $\tilde{\mathbf{m}}$. The second term, $\pm\sum_{i,f'} s_i^{(f')}$, is expected to determine the correlation value independent of the image content. The $\pm$ notation indicates the sign of the product obtained by multiplying $\tilde{m}_i$ and m_i. If the embedded bit value is 1, the sign is plus; if it is 0, the sign is minus.

Step 4: Determine bit value b by comparing correlation value c with threshold value $T(>0)$:

$$b = \begin{cases} 1 & \text{if } c \geq T \\ 0 & \text{if } c \leq -T \\ \text{"not detected"} & \text{if } -T < c < T. \end{cases} \tag{4}$$

3.3   Prototype

We developed a prototype system with a standard video interface for video WM embedding using a PC with a video I/O board, an NTSC video camera, and an NTSC monitor. Figure 5 shows an external view of the system. The system specifications are shown in Table 1.

The system captures the NTSC video signals output from the video camera, embeds WMs into the frames, and outputs the signal to the monitor in NTSC output. The WMs represent 64 bits of information and are embedded into the luminance component (Y) of the video signal during I/O. The WM embedding and I/O are done in real time.

Fig. 5. Prototype of improved real-time WM embedding system

Table 1. Prototype system specifications

PC	Ordinary PC with video capture board CPU: Intel® Xeon™ 2.4 GHz[1] Memory: 1GB RAM
Interface	NTSC input/output
Video in	Video camera
Video out	TV monitor
Resolution	640 ×480 pixels (VGA)
Frame rate	29.97 fps
WM payload	64 bits of information

4   Evaluation

4.1   Measured Performance Time Inside System

The prototype system has five processing steps (Table 2), and the time taken for each was measured. In step 1, the WM embedding process is initialized (memory allocation, WM pattern generation, etc.). In step 2, the device driver for the video I/O board is initialized. The input video stream can now be captured by the system. In step 3, the frame receiving process captures a video frame and synchronously places it into internal memory. In step 4, a WM is embedded in the frame data. In step 5, the frame sending process saves the embedded frame into the output video buffer.

The processing times for each step was measured internally and written to a log file while the video was streaming. As shown by the results in Table 2, the processing was done in real-time. The times for the three iterative steps, 3–5, are the averages for 100 frames. Only the times for 100 frames were logged to prevent the log file from becoming too large, which would result in new entries being cached in the hard-disk buffer and then flushed out by the PC's operating system. Our application program is unable to control the hard-disk buffer, and, since cache flushing is unpredictable, it would disturb our measurements. Therefore, we avoided long-term measurement.

---

[1] Intel® and Xeon™ are trademarks or registered trademarks of Intel Corporation or its subsidiaries in the United States and other countries.

In real-time processing, each frame should be processed in 33 ms on average because the video data is streamed at 29.97 fps. Since the total average time for the three iterative steps was 32 ms/frame, real-time processing is feasible. Contrary to expectations, the CPU load of the prototype was not particularly high in step 3. The reason the frame receiving time was so long is attributed to synchronization, i.e. waiting for video input. The output SDTV video stream appeared natural on the basis of glancing at the TV monitor.

Table 2. Processing time

Step	Process	Time
1	WM process initialization	54 ms
2	Video I/O initialization	721 ms
3	Frame receiving	20 ms / frame
4	WM embedding (VGA)	1 ms / frame
5	Frame sending	11 ms / frame

4.2   Measured Performance Time Outside System

Although the logged data demonstrated that the WM embedding was done in real time, this is insufficient for evaluating overall system performance. Once the frame-sending process (step 5) is finished, it is assumed that the video I/O board converts the frame data into an output video signal. However, if a frame in a long video stream is dropped and replaced with the immediately preceding frame, which is stored in the board's buffer, the log file may not reflect this. If the output board does not handle errors reliably, there may be no interruption event in the application software. The frame rate of the output signal is regulated to 29.97 fps, that is, the video stream must carry 29.97 frames per second. Even if only one frame is dropped, the actual frame-rate will be less than 29.97 fps. It is difficult to detect frame drops by glancing at a TV monitor.

We thus conducted a test to confirm that the processing could be done in real time, that is, that a WM-embedded SDTV video signal could be output at 29.97 fps. The test was done from outside the WM-embedding system using a five-step process, as illustrated in Figure 6.

1. A visible sequence code pattern was overwritten into each frame image (see left image in Figure 7).
2. The frames were written onto a DVD-Video disc. A DVD player then sent the frames in an SDTV video signal to the test system.
3. The test system embedded an invisible WM into every frame and output them in an SDTV video signal to a monitoring PC in real time.
4. The monitoring PC captured the visibly and invisibly marked video data and encoded it (QVGA, MPEG1) using lossy compression and wrote it to a file at 1 Mbps. The deduced image size and bit rate reflect the performance limits of the monitoring PC in this experiment.

5. The visible code patterns in the monitored data were compared with the originals. If a frame had been dropped, the resulting difference in patterns made it easy to detect. Even when dropped frames were difficult to visibly detect due to little movement in the original images, the pattern differences made them easy to find.

Testing three times using 300–313 continuous frames confirmed that the processing could be done in real time, i.e., the estimated frame rate was 29.97 fps while about 10 seconds. Although the video frames were for 15 seconds, about 5 seconds was consumed by manual operations, i.e., pushing the play and record buttons in a synchronous manner.

If a mismatch in patterns revealed a frame drop, the step in which it was dropped could not be pinpointed as drops can occur in steps 2, 3, and 4 due to unforeseen events. However, no frame drops were detected in this experiment.

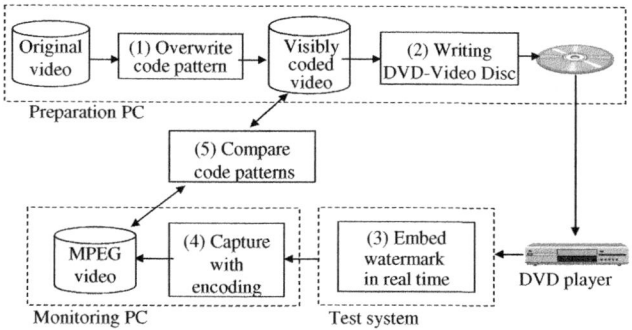

Fig. 6. Testing using sequence code patterns

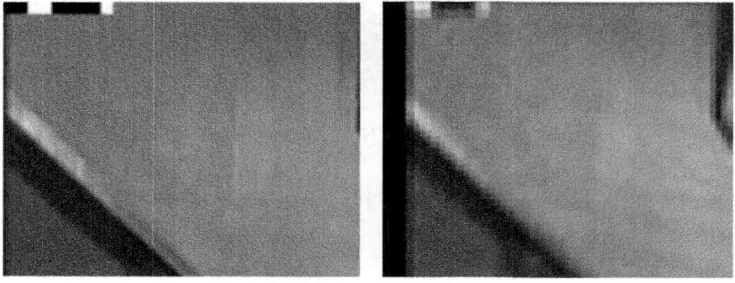

Fig. 7. Visible sequence code pattern written into frame image. Left image is original with pattern overwritten at the top left. Right image is same image after processing and capturing by monitoring PC. Black line down left of processed image was added during capture (step 4).

4.3   Image Quality

We subjectively evaluated the quality of images watermarked with our improved system using a procedure based on Recommendation ITU-R BT.500-7 [15]. Watermarked videos were displayed on a monitor and evaluated by ten participants, who rated the image quality using the scale shown in Table 3.

A test in which both original and watermarked content is displayed in real time is difficult to arrange. Strict evaluation of image quality requires the use of dedicated equipment such as an uncompressed video disk recorder. Moreover, it is difficult to correctly operate analog video devices in a synchronous manner when testing multiple items.

Therefore, we manually embedded WMs into video files using the same program libraries as those in the proposed system and then encoded the files (MPEG2, 8 Mbps). The evaluators compared the original contents with the watermarked ones for both the previous system [8] and the improved system. The videos were the same as those used previously [8–10] (see Figure 8).

As shown in Table 4, the average scores with the improved system were virtually the same as those with the previous one, indicating that the image quality had been maintained.

Table 3. Level of disturbance and rating scale

Disturbance	Score
Imperceptible	5
Perceptible but not annoying	4
Slightly annoying	3
Annoying	2
Very annoying	1

(a)	(b)	(c)

Fig. 8. Scenes from sample videos: (a) EntranceHall, (b) WalkThroughTheSquare, (c) WhaleShow

Table 4. Subjective image quality

Sample	Original	Improved
EntranceHall	4.9	5.0
WalkThroughTheSquare	4.9	4.9
WhaleShow	4.7	4.7

The peak signal noise ratios (PSNRs) calculated for the three sample videos (EntranceHall, WalkThroughTheSquare, and WhaleShow) were respectively 33.8, 28.9, and 32.3 dB, as shown in the first column in Table 5, when uncompressed watermarked images and uncompressed original images are compared. The MPEG2 encoder created noises in the encoded original videos, resulting in PSNRs of 28.1 to 33.3, as shown in the second column. The values for the encoded WMed videos were at almost the same level as those for the encoded original videos, as shown in the third column. The noise caused by the watermarking is thus somewhat veiled by the encoder noise. In other words, the WM strength was properly set so that the watermarks were almost imperceptible to the human eye. The same WM strength was also used in the WM robustness test.

Table 5. Quantative image quality (PSNR)

Sample	Not-encoded WMed video (dB)	Encoded original video (dB)	Encoded WMed video (dB)
EntranceHall	33.8	33.3	33.8
WalkThroughTheSquare	28.9	28.1	28.0
WhaleShow	32.3	28.4	28.3

4.4   Watermark Robustness

Although the proposed WM-embedding system speeds up the process by executing a pre-process common to every video frame in advance and then a post-process specific to each frame, its WM robustness is theoretically equal to that of the base method [11].

WM robustness was evaluated using the same videos, which have various motion properties used in image quality evaluation. We used the WM detection ratio, which is the ratio of the number of points where the embedded 64 bits were correctly detected to the total number of detection points. There were 450 frames in total for each video. For instance, if the WMs of 30 sequential frames were detected at a time (n = 30), there were 15 detection points in each video.

A WM was correctly detected at each point. That is, the detection ratio was 100% for all three samples (VGA, MPEG2, 8Mbps). These results show that the WMed images satisfied the two essential requirements: the WMs should not degrade image quality, and they should be robust enough to be reliably detected after common video processing.

The improved system has a general-purpose interface, meaning that the output signal can be connected to a video encoder with a lower compression rate. We therefore evaluated WM robustness against representative video encodings: MPEG2 and H.264 (MPEG4/AVC (Advanced Video Codec)). One of the WMed video stream samples (Figure 8 (b)) was encoded using MPEG2 or H.264 at two different bit rates (MPEG2: 3 and 4 Mbps; H.264: 700 kbps and 1 Mbps). The number of accumulated frames is n as described in section 3.2. The detection ratios for n = 1, 5, 10, and 30 from 450 frames of watermarked images are shown in Figure 9. When n = 30, detection ratios for MPEG2 and H.264 video are 100%. That is, WMs can be detected from one-second video (30 frames) in this experiment.

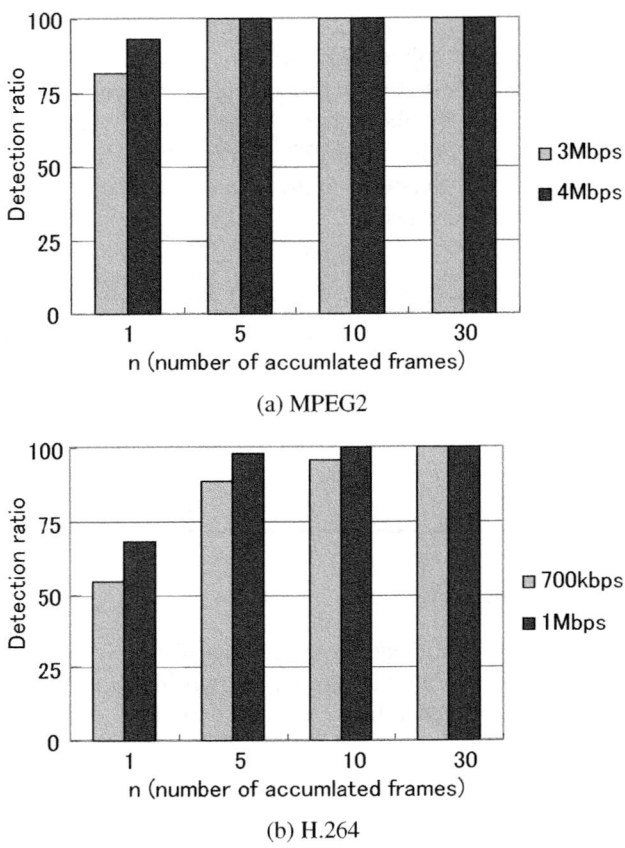

(a) MPEG2

(b) H.264

Fig. 9. Watermark detection ratios for n = 1, 5, 10, and 30 from 450 frames of watermarked images. MPEG2 (a) and H.264 (b) were used for video encoding.

4.5   Further Applications

The improved system has three major advantages (resolution, codec, and output), compared with the previous one [8]. Its use of VGA, which is used more widely than QVGA, extends the range of potential applications, as shown in Table 6.

While the previous system is theoretically applicable to various services such as video streaming for mobile phones and narrow-band PCs, the actual system requires the use of a specific format for the data files. Customization is required to change the output method or file formats. Since the improved system is independent of the codec and output, the codec can be switched by simply moving the output connecter from one encoder to another encoder or to a disk recorder. The signal can also be split for use in several devices.

Potential applications of the improved system include copy management, video authentication, and copyright protection, as shown in Table 6. For instance, it could be used to embed serial numbers in video package copies, which would enable them to be identified so that illegal copies could be tracked. It could be used to embed authentication information such as time stamps in videos, which would enable authentication of archived videos from surveillance cameras and of lectures, medical operations, early art works, and interviews.

Deployment of such applications has not been cost-effective, so small businesses must take the lead in deploying them. Hardware-based systems [3-5] would be costly to implement, so software-based system running on a PC would be more attractive. Although a software-based system running on a PC has been investigated [7], implementing a system that uses a specific platform may encounter a compatibility problem. Users may hesitate to replace their existing PCs with new ones for running WM software. Our software-based system running on a PC is practical because it does not require costly dedicated hardware and because it is independent of the platform used for parallel computing. Moreover, industrial testing of real-time processing performance demonstrated that out proposed system is reliable and useful.

Table 6. Improved versus previous system

	Previous system [8]	Improved system
Resolution	QVGA	VGA
Codec	MPEG4-dependent	Independent
Output	Files on HDD	Video signal (SDTV)
Potential applications	- Video streaming for mobile phones and narrowband PCs - Thumbnail videos Video clips for rough editing	- Same targets + - Managing video package copies - Authenticating archived videos (e.g. records of surveillance camera, lectures, medical operations, early art works, and live interviews)

5   Alternate Implementation Based on Different Watermarking Algorithm

In section 3, we described our proposed implementation technique, which enables real-time watermarking of SDTV video, using an early watermarking algorithm. In this section, we discuss the general effectiveness of the proposed implementation technique using a more up-to-date watermarking algorithm. The new implementation is the same as that described in section 3 except for the use of a different watermarking algorithm.

5.1   Algorithm Used

The algorithm used here embeds robust video watermarks that are immune to not only rotation, scaling, and translation but also to random geometric distortion and any of their combinations [17]. Watermarks are embedded in two constituent planes (U and V) of each color frame of the video.

[WM embedding]

The two color-difference sets for the f -th color frame consisting of W×H-pixels are $\mathbf{U}^f = \{U_{i,j}^f \mid 1 \le i \le W, 1 \le j \le H\}$ and $\mathbf{V}^f = \{V_{i,j}^f \mid 1 \le i \le W, 1 \le j \le H\}$. A mask, $\mathbf{M} = \{M_{i,j} \mid 1 \le i \le L, 1 \le j \le L\}$ comprising pseudo random noise sequences of integers +1 and -1, is used to indicate the existence of a WM. The bit value of the embedded information is b. WM strength α is previously set adequately. $\mathbf{U}^f$, $\mathbf{V}^f$, b, α, and the pseudo random noise for $\mathbf{M}$ are input parameters for the WM embedding process. The Y plane is not modified.

The WM pattern for the U plane is generated by simply multiplying each element of the mask by WM strength α. That for the V plane is generated by shifting and reversing the mask in accordance with the bit value of the embedded information, b. The shift vector is $\mathbf{sv} = (sv, sv)$. The output parameters, that is, the WMed color-difference sets for the f -th frame are $\mathbf{U}'^f = \{U_{i,j}'^f \mid 1 \le i \le W, 1 \le j \le H\}$ and $\mathbf{V}'^f = \{V_{i,j}'^f \mid 1 \le i \le W, 1 \le j \le H\}$. When one-bit is embedded, these outputs are obtained in accordance with

$$U_{i,j}'^f = U_{i,j}^f + \alpha M_{i,j},$$

$$V_{i,j}'^f = \begin{cases} V_{i,j}^f + \alpha M_{i-sv, j-sv} & \text{if } b=1 \\ V_{i,j}^f - \alpha M_{i-sv, j-sv} & \text{if } b=0 \end{cases} \qquad (5)$$

[WM detection]

Calculate correlation value c' using

$$c' = \frac{1}{WH} \sum_{i,j} \left(U_{i,j} - \overline{U} \right)\left(V_{i+sv, j+sv} - \overline{V} \right), \qquad (6)$$

where $\overline{U}$ is the average value of $U_{i,j}$ over i and j, $\overline{V}$ is the average value of $V_{i,j}$ over i and j. Shift vector $\mathbf{sv}$ is the same as that used in the embedding process. If $c' > 0$, b is detected as 1; if $c' < 0$, b is detected as 0; if $c' = 0$, b is not detected.

5.2   Measured Performance

Using our proposed implementation technique, as described in section 3.2, we make the watermark-pattern generation process common to every frame a pre-process and reuse the WM-pattern output from this pre-process. That is, each of the two WM-patterns for the U and V planes are added to each plane in every frame in real-time processing. The WM payload is 64 bits, the same as that for the implementation described in section 3.

The YUV422 format is used for handling video frames in the alternate implementation. The data quantity ratio for the Y, U, and V planes is 4:2:2. Each element data in the U and V planes takes one sample from two pixels that are aligned horizontally in a frame. The total data size for both the U and V planes is therefore the same as that for the Y plane, which is used in the implementation described in section 3.

As a result, real-time WM embedding was achieved using a different algorithm [17]. The total time for processing each frame (step 3, 4, and 5) was no more than 33 ms per a frame, as shown in Table 7. Moreover, glancing at a monitor revealed that no frames were dropped.

The processing time for step 2 (video I/O initialization of the U and V planes) was 1851 ms, as shown in Table 7, which is more than the 721 ms for the Y plane (Table 2). The processing times for step 3 (frame receiving) was less (10 vs. 20 ms) while that for step 5 (frame sending) was greater (16 vs. 11 ms). The shorter time for frame receiving is attributed to a reduced waiting period for synchronization while the longer time for frame sending is attributed to a longer waiting period for synchronization. One possible reason for this longer waiting period is that the memory-access efficiencies for the U and V planes differ from that for the Y plane, but this cannot be confirmed because the video board specifications regarding this are unavailable.

Table 7. Processing time with alternate implementation

Step	Process	Time
1	WM process initialization	9 ms
2	Video I/O initialization	1851 ms
3	Frame receiving	10 ms / frame
4	WM embedding (U, V planes)	6 ms / frame
5	Frame sending	16 ms / frame

5.3 Image Quality and Robustness

The algorithm used in the alternate implementation is based on the characteristic of human vision that color changes are less perceptible than luminance changes and was previously shown to satisfy the essential requirements for image quality and WM robustness [17].

As described in the previous report [17], image quality of the WMed images was subjectively evaluated on the basis of ITU-R BT.500-7 [15]. The results for the three samples (720×480 pixels, 300 frames) showed that image quality depends on the WM strength. A strength of 4.50 to 4.91 resulted in a quality level 4 ("Perceptible but not annoying"). Moreover, WMs with this strength were shown to be robust against rotation, scaling, transformation, and random geometric distortion (and any combination thereof).

6   Conclusion

Real-time video watermark (WM) embedding is essential for live content distribution. While our previous real-time WM embedding system, which uses software running on an ordinary PC, is suitable for content distribution, it generates only MPEG-4 encoded WMed files and handles only QVGA format, which is converted from the VGA format of the incoming video. Moreover, it stores the encoded files on hard disk and has no video interface with distribution servers.

Our improved version has a standard video interface, can directly handle the VGA format of the incoming video signal, and is separate from the encoding process. It can thus be incorporated into various types encoding and distribution systems. Real-time processing is achieved by making the WM-pattern generation process common to every frame a pre-process, by reusing the WM pattern output from this pre-process, and by storing the WMed video frames in video memory on the video I/O board, thereby eliminating the need for storing them in buffers on hard disk. This WM embedding method is independent of the parallel-computing platform. Evaluation of the prototype system demonstrated the validity of this approach in terms of performance time, WMed image quality and WM robustness to video processing.

References

1. Cox, I., Miller, M., Bloom, J., Fridrich, J., Kalker, T.: Digital Watermarking and Steganography. Morgan Kaufmann Publishers Inc., San Francisco (2007)
2. Jeong, Y.J., Kim, W.H., Moon, K.S., Kim, J.N.: Implementation of Watermark Detection System for Hardware Based Video Watermark Embedder. In: Proc. of Int'l Conf. on Convergence and Hybrid Information Technology, pp. 450–453 (2008)
3. Mathai, J.N., Sheikholeslami, A., Kundur, D.: VLSI Implementation of a Real-Time Video Watermark Embedder and Detector. In: Proc. of IEEE Int'l Symposium on Circuits and Systems, vol. 2, pp. II-772 – II-775 (2003)
4. Garimella, A., Satyanarayana, M., Murugesh, P., Niranjan, U.: ASIC for Digital Color Image Watermarking. In: Proc. of IEEE Signal Processing Education Workshop, pp. 292–296 (2004)
5. Terada, K., Fujikawa, Y., Fujii, Y., Echizen, I., Yoshiura, H., Nishioka, K., Bandou, T.: Development of Real-time Video Watermarking System Using Media Processor. Journal of the Institute of Image Information and Television Engineers (ITE) 58(12), 1820–1827 (2004)
6. Chen, Y.-K., Holliman, M., Debes, E., Zheltov, S., Knyazev, A., Bratanov, S., Belenov, R., Santos, I.: Media Applications on Hyper-Threading Technology. Intel. Technology Journal Q1 6(1), 56–69 (2002)
7. Kim, K.S., Lee, H.Y., Im, D.H., Lee, H.K.: Practical, Real-time, and Robust Watermarking on the Spatial Domain for High-Definition Video Contents. IEICE Transactions on Information and Systems E91-D(5), 1359–1368 (2008)
8. Echizen, I., Yamada, T., Fujii, Y., Tezuka, S., Yoshiura, H.: Real-time Video Watermark Embedding System using Software on Personal Computer. In: Proc. of IEEE Int'l Conf. on Systems, Man and Cybernetics (SMC 2005), pp. 3369–3373 (2005)

9. Echizen, I., Tanimoto, K., Yamada, T., Dainaka, M., Tezuka, S., Yoshiura, H.: PC-based Real-Time Watermark Embedding System with Standard Video Interface. In: Proc. of IEEE Int'l Conf. on Systems, Man and Cybernetics (SMC 2006), pp. 267–271 (2006)
10. Yamada, T., Takahashi, Y., Yoshiura, H., Echizen, I.: Evaluation of PC-based Real-Time Watermark Embedding System for Standard-Definition Video Stream. In: Tsihrintzis, G.A., Virvou, M., Howlett, R.J., Jain, L.C. (eds.) Int'l Sym. on Intelligent Interactive Multimedia Systems and Services (KES IIMSS 2008), New Directions in Intelligent Interactive Multimedia. SCI, vol. 142, pp. 331–340. Springer, Heidelberg (2008)
11. Bender, W., Gruhl, D., Morimoto, N.: Techniques for Data Hiding. In: Proc. SPIE, vol. 2420, pp. 165–173 (1995)
12. Delaigle, J.F., De Vleeschouwer, C., Macq, B.: Watermarking Algorithm Based on a Human Visual Model. Signal Processing 66, 319–335 (1998)
13. Kundur, D., Hatzinakos, D.: Digital Watermarking using Multiresolution Wavelet Decomposition. In: Int'l. Conf. on Acoustics, Speech and Signal Processing, vol. 5, pp. 2969–2972 (1998)
14. Echizen, I., Yoshiura, H., Arai, T., Kimura, H., Takeuchi, T.: General Quality Maintenance Module for Motion Picture Watermarking. IEEE Trans. Consumer Electronics 45(4), 1150–1158 (1999)
15. Rec. ITU-R BT.500-7, Methodology for the Subjective Assessment of the Quality of Television Pictures (1995)
16. Hartung, F., Girod, B.: Watermarking of Uncompressed and Compressed Video. Signal Processing 66(3), 283–301 (1998)
17. Atomori, Y., Echizen, I., Dainaka, M., Nakayama, S., Yoshiura, H.: Robust Video Watermarking based on Dual-plane Correlation for Immunity to Rotation, Scale, Translation, and Random Distortion. Journal of Digital Information Management 6(2), 161–167 (2008)

IR Hiding: Method for Preventing Illegal Recording of Videos Based on Differences in Sensory Perception between Humans and Devices

Isao Echizen[1,3], Takayuki Yamada[1], and Seiichi Gohshi[2]

[1] Graduate University for Advanced Studies, Japan
[2] Sharp Ltd., Display Systems Laboratories, Japan
[3] National Institute of Informatics, Japan
iechizen@nii.ac.jp

Abstract. A method is described that prevents videos and movies displayed on a screen from being illegally recorded using digital cameras and camcorders. Conventional protection methods, such as embedding digital watermarks into images for use in identifying where and when the original content was illegally recorded, do not actually prevent the content from being illegally recorded. The proposed method, which is based on the differences in sensory characteristics between humans and devices, actually prevents illegal recording. It does not require the addition of a function to the user-side device; instead, it uses infrared light to corrupt the recorded content. This light is invisible to the naked eye but is picked up by the CCD or CMOS device in the camera. This makes the recorded content unusable. Testing using a functional prototype implemented on a 100-inch cinema screen showed that the method effectively prevents illegal recording. Also described is an effective countermeasure against the use of a camera or camcorder fitted with an infrared cut filter.

Keywords: Copyright protection, Sensory perception, Infrared LED, Bartley effect.

1 Introduction

High-quality digital content, such as images and videos shot by individuals, is now widely available because of the rapid growth in broadband networks and the popularity of high-performance consumer audio/video equipment. Anyone these days can easily shoot videos using camcorders and distribute the recorded content via the Internet. A serious problem, however, is copyright violation of non-personal content such as videos and movies displayed on digital signage; such content can easily be illegally recorded using a cell phone's digital camera or a camcorder and distributed via the Internet or sold illegally on recording media such as DVDs. The Motion Picture Association of America (MPAA) [1] estimates the damage caused by illegal recording of copyrighted films to be three billion dollars per year [2]. This estimate takes into consideration advances in camcorder technology that have enabled better quality recordings. Preventing illegal recording of videos and movies is thus essential

Y.Q. Shi (Ed.): Transactions on DHMS VII, LNCS 7110, pp. 34–51, 2012.

for copyright protection. Digital watermarks can be used to trace the illegal distribution of digital content [3–7], but they cannot prevent someone from illegally recording films in a movie theater with a camcorder.

This paper describes a method for stopping the illegal recording of videos and movies using digital cameras or camcorders, It uses near-infrared (IR) signals to corrupt the recorded content. These noise signals cannot be seen by the human eye but are picked up by image sensors such as charge coupled devices (CCDs) and complementary metal-oxide semiconductors (CMOSs). A new function does not need to be added to the user-side device. We developed a prototype system for preventing the illegal recording of films in movie theaters that uses near-IR light emitting diodes (LEDs) placed on the back side of a 100-inch cinema screen. The results of an experiment demonstrated that this method effectively prevents illegal recording.

This paper focuses on both the theoretical and practical aspects of our proposed method. Section 2 describes conventional approaches and the related problems. Section 3 introduces our method based on the differences in sensory characteristics between humans and devices. Sections 4 and 5 describe our prototype system and the results of our experimental evaluation. Section 6 describes a simple countermeasure against illegal recording using an IR-cut filter, which can eliminate the noise, and describes the prototype developed for detecting such a filter. Section 7 briefly summarizes the key points of this paper.

2 Conventional Approaches

Digital rights management (DRM) is a common approach to preventing unauthorized copying of digital content. It aims to provide persistent access control by encrypting the content and allowing access (e.g., play, view, change, or copy) only by authorized users or devices, i.e., ones with the decryption key [8]. For instance, content such as video data on commercial DVDs is usually encrypted with the Content Scramble System [9] and can only be decrypted and displayed by DVD players with the decryption key. However, when that content is shown on a screen or display, it can be illegally recorded by using a digital camera or camcorder, thereby bypassing the protection offered by DRM. Preventing the illegal recording of content shown on screens or displays is thus essential for preventing copyright violation.

In the digital watermarking approach, a watermark containing identifying information is embedded into the content. By extracting the information from the watermark, an investigator can identify where and when the original content was illegally recorded [3–7]. Various watermarking methods have been studied, including embedding such information as the theater ID into movie frames to trace the flow of illegally recorded content [3–5], using spread-spectrum audio watermarking for multichannel movie sound tracks to estimate the position in the theater of a camcorder being used for recording [6], and using spread-spectrum video watermarking with auto-correlation to estimate the recording position from the distorted coordinates of recorded watermarked video [7]. Although digital watermarking psychologically dampens the motivation to illegally record videos, it does not actually prevent illegal recording. Moreover, content creators are apparently reluctant to add watermarks to their content due to a strong feeling of attachment to their work.

Our proposed method overcomes these problems by directly preventing the illegal recording of videos and movies using camcorders. It is based on the differences in sensory characteristics between humans and devices. It uses IR light to corrupt the recorded content with noise signals that are invisible to the naked eye but are picked up by the CCD or CMOS device of a camera used for illegal recording, thus obviating the need for embedding watermarks into the content or adding a new function to the user-side device.

An approach similar in concept to that of the proposed method was considered by Bourdon et al. [10]. They theoretically investigated the use of spatial and temporal modulation of projected light to prevent illegal recording in movie theaters. An experimental evaluation to validate this approach was not conducted. Moreover, such an approach could be circumvented by manually controlling the camcorder's shutter speed. We are unaware of any other approaches similar to ours.

3   Proposed Method

3.1   Principle

As mentioned, our method for preventing the illegal recording of videos and movies is based on the differences in sensory characteristics between humans and devices. Figure 1 illustrates the perceptible areas of the sensory perceptions of humans and sensor devices (e.g. the human eye and CCD or human ear and microphone). Sensor devices have been developed in such a way that their pick-up characteristics correspond to humans' visual/auditory perceptions. However, certain design limitations make it impossible for their characteristics to completely match those of human visual perception.

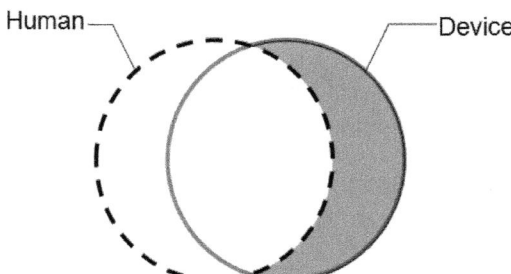

Fig. 1. Illustration of how sensory perceptions of humans and sensor devices overlap but do not correspond

Our proposed method prevents the illegal recording of videos and movies by adding a noise signal to the shaded area in the figure, which corresponds to light wavelengths that humans cannot see but to which sensor devices can react. The noise signal is created within the display (projection screen or liquid crystal display (LCD)); that is, our method does not require new functions to be added to the camera user's equipment.

3.2   Differences in Sensory Characteristics

According to the International Commission on Illumination, the wavelengths of visible light are between 380 and 780 nm [11] while those that can be picked up by image sensor devices, such as CCDs and CMOSs used in digital cameras and camcorders, are between 200 and 1100 nm. Digital camcorders were designed to react to signals with wavelengths outside the visible range to give them the high level of luminous sensitivity needed for shooting in the dark. Figure 2 illustrates the wavelength ranges of the human visual system and camcorders.

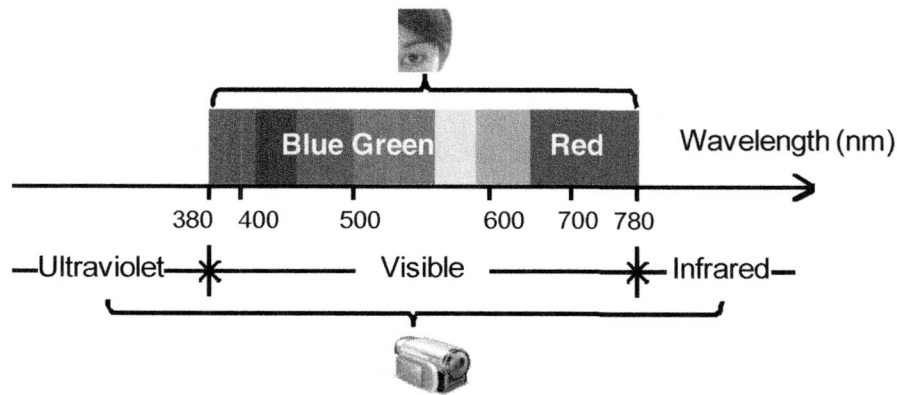

Fig. 2. Wavelength ranges of human visual system and digital video cameras

The stimulus values for the human eye, B_H, G_H, and R_H, and the response values for a digital camcorder, B_D, G_D, and R_D, are thus given by

$$B_H = \int_{380}^{780} s(\lambda)\,\overline{b}(\lambda)d\lambda$$

$$G_H = \int_{380}^{780} s(\lambda)\cdot\overline{g}(\lambda)d\lambda \tag{1}$$

$$R_H = \int_{380}^{780} s(\lambda)\cdot\overline{r}(\lambda)d\lambda$$

$$B_D = \int_{200}^{1100} s(\lambda)\,b(\lambda)d\lambda$$

$$G_D = \int_{200}^{1100} s(\lambda)\cdot g(\lambda)d\lambda \tag{2}$$

$$R_D = \int_{200}^{1100} s(\lambda)\cdot r(\lambda)d\lambda$$

where $s(\lambda)$ is the source of a signal with wavelength λ, $\overline{b}(\lambda)$, $\overline{g}(\lambda)$, and $\overline{r}(\lambda)$ are the color matching functions, and $b(\lambda)$, $g(\lambda)$, and $r(\lambda)$ are the spectrum products of a digital camcorder (including the spectrum sensitivity and transmission spectrum of the image sensor) [11–14]. We denote the noise signal and the light source of the video to be displayed on a screen or monitor as $n(\lambda,t)$ and $v(\lambda,t)$, respectively. The source of the signal for the proposed method is given by

$$s(\lambda,t) = v(\lambda,t) + n(\lambda,t) \tag{3}$$

The relationship between each stimulus value of the human eye and the corresponding response value of a digital camcorder is given by

$$X_H[s(\lambda,t)] = X_H[v(\lambda,t)] \tag{4}$$

$$X_D[s(\lambda,t)] \neq X_D[v(\lambda,t)] \tag{5}$$

where X represents R, G, or B. That is, the human eye perceives $s(\lambda,t)$ and $v(\lambda,t)$ to be the same whereas the digital camcorder recognizes [picks up] the difference. The difference between $s(\lambda,t)$ and $v(\lambda,t)$ is

$$\Delta = |X_D[s(\lambda,t)] - X_D[v(\lambda,t)]| \tag{6}$$

from which we can derive

$$\Delta = |X_D[n(\lambda,t)]| \tag{7}$$

using the linearity of formula (2). In the following two sections, we analyze the wavelength and time characteristics of noise signal $n(\lambda,t)$ used to increase the above difference.

3.3   Wavelength of Noise Signal

The wavelength of the noise signal must be outside the visible range to prevent it being noticed by a viewer. Note that IR radiation is electromagnetic radiation with a longer wavelength than visible light whereas ultraviolet (UV) radiation is electromagnetic radiation with a shorter wavelength. Since UV radiation can seriously damage human skin, eyes, and immune system, it is not a suitable noise signal. IR radiation, on the other hand, is widely used in various types of consumer equipment such as TV remote controls and heaters, and its safety has been established. LEDs, laser diodes, xenon lamps, and halogen lamps are IR light emitters. We chose IR LEDs because they are inexpensive. Unlike lasers, which emit on a single wavelength, LEDs emit on multiple wavelengths distributed on a Gaussian curve. Therefore, the human eye perceives them as emitting red if the peak wavelength is close to the human visible range. Conversely, their noise effect on content recorded using a digital camcorder decreases as the peak wavelength moves away from the visible range. We evaluated the noise effect and perceivability of IR LED light at five peak wavelengths (780, 810, 850, 870, and 940 nm) when viewed by the naked eye and in recordings made using two digital camcorders (1/6-inch CCD-based and 1/3.2-inch CMOS-based). The results showed that the IR LED light with a peak wavelength of 870 nm had the strongest noise effect and was the least perceivable to the naked eye.

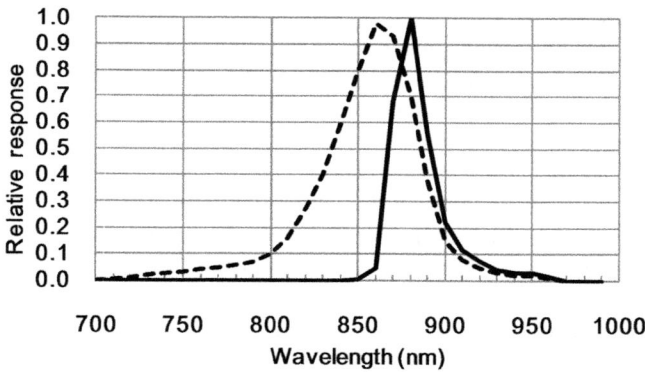

Fig. 3. Distributions of relative response (dashed line: IR LED light with peak wavelength of 870 nm; solid line: IR LED light filtered by short-wavelength cut filter with cut-on wavelength of 870 nm)

As shown by the distribution of the relative response of the infrared LED light with a peak wavelength of 870 nm in Figure 3, the emissions were mostly shorter than 780 nm, which is the upper limit of the human visible range, so they would cause negligible visual degradation. To avoid even this slight degradation, we used a short-wavelength cut filter with a cut-on wavelength of 870 nm (cut ratio of 50%). As shown by the solid line in the figure, the emissions causing visual degradation were thereby eliminated while the peak wavelength at which the digital camcorder reacted was only slightly longer. On the basis of these results, we used IR LEDs with a peak wavelength of 870 nm and short-wavelength cut filters with a cut-on wavelength of 870 nm.

3.4   Time Characteristics of Noise Signal

We must also consider the temporal characteristics of the noise signal. Bartley showed that humans perceive the signal from a flashing light most easily when its frequency is around 10 Hz [15]. Moreover, Talbot's law says that humans perceive a continuous light with an average intensity rather than a flashing light when the frequency of the flashing light is sufficiently high [15]. Accordingly, we used a noise signal flashing at around 10 Hz in order to increase the disturbance of the recorded content.

3.5   Safety of IR LEDs

LEDs were initially listed under the safety standard for lasers (IEC 60825-1: Safety of laser products - Part 1: Equipment classification and requirements, 1993). This standard was too severe as subsequently shown by various experimental evaluations. LEDs were eliminated from this restrictive standard in 2006.

4   Prototype

Figures 4 and 5 respectively show an overview and the structure of the prototype system we developed for illegal recording prevention and implemented on a 100-inch cinema screen. The system is comprised of two circuits: a flashing regulator circuit and an IR emission circuit.

Flashing Regulator Circuit

The flashing regulator circuit generates a flashing signal between 1 and 64 Hz by transmitting pulses from a crystal oscillator to a frequency demultiplier. These pulses are used to flash the IR LEDs in the emission circuit.

IR Emission Circuit

The IR emission circuit has nine infrared emission units, which are mounted in a 3 by 3 grid behind the screen. Each unit has 18 IR LEDs, a short-wavelength cut filter, a cooling fan attached to the front and back sides of the LEDs, and a DC power supply. Each unit consumes 36 W of electrical power. A cinema screen has many tiny holes (~1 mm in diameter) for letting sound from the back speakers pass through, and the IR light output from this circuit also passes through these holes.

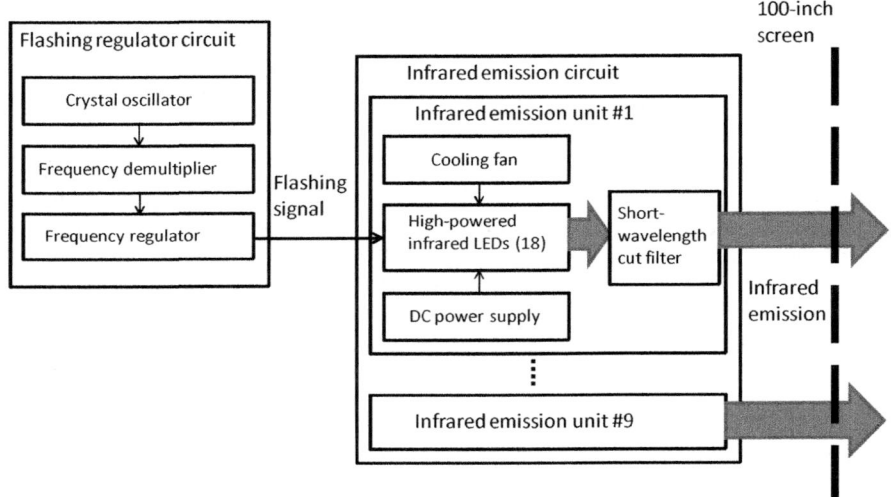

Fig. 4. System structure

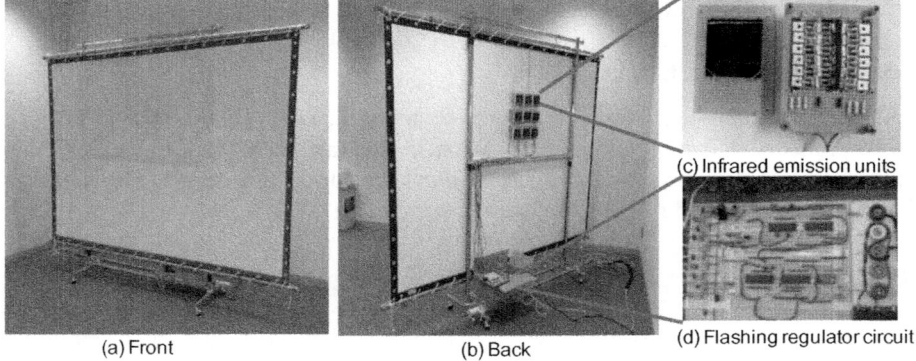

Fig. 5. System overview

5   Evaluation

We subjectively evaluated the quality of videos displayed using the prototype system using the procedure described in ITU Recommendation BT.500 [16]. More precisely, we selected 6 samples from the 30 standard video samples [17] and displayed them on the screen with the proposed method (prototype system) and without it (normal system). Fifteen evaluators subjectively evaluated the level of disturbance with the prototype system against that with the normal system for two cases: (a) viewing of the original videos and (b) viewing of the same videos recorded using two different ordinary digital camcorders and a cell phone equipped with a digital camera. The aim in case (a) was that the evaluators would not perceive any visual degradation in the videos shown with the prototype system. The aim in case (b), on the other hand, was that the level of disturbance in the videos would be as high as possible. Table 1 summarizes the evaluation conditions.

5.1   Standards for Subjective Evaluation

Standards for subjective evaluations can be classified into two types: evaluations defined by the International Telecommunication Union Radio Communications Sector (ITU-R) [18] and those defined by the International Telecommunication Union Telecommunication Standardization Sector (ITU-T) [19]. ITU-R type evaluations are intended for high-quality videos for broadcast. ITU-T type evaluations, on the other hand, are intended for videos for multimedia communication using videophones and video conferencing systems. Since our prototype system is intended for films in theaters, we used an ITU-R type evaluation.

ITU-R evaluations can be classified into two types: double-stimulus continuous quality-scale (DSCQS) for evaluating the level of visual degradation in videos on communication channels and double-stimulus impairment scale (DSIS) for evaluating the level of visual disturbance in videos.

Table 1. Evaluation conditions

Screen	100-inch cinema screen
Projector	Digital projector (1000 ANSI lumen)
Video	NHK Engineering Services, Inc.
	6 samples selected from 30 standard video samples (Fig. 6)
	Swinging
	Flamingoes
	Buddhist images
	Driving
	Skyscrapers
	View from sky with credits
Recorders	1/3.2-inch CMOS-based digital camcorder (207 M pixel)
	1/6-inch CCD-based digital camcorder (69 M pixel)
	Cellular phone with CMOS-based digital camera (8 M pixel)
Flashing frequency	continuous, 5, 10, 15, and 20 Hz
Evaluators	15 non-specialists

Since the noise signal of the prototype system can be considered to be a disturbance in video, we used the DSIS standard so that the evaluators could subjectively evaluate the level of disturbance.

5.2   Evaluated Video Samples

The six selected samples represent various camera actions (zooming and panning), object movements (slow and quick), and image processing particular to films (video with credits), as shown in Figure 6.

- **Swinging:** Zoomed-in scene of woman on a swing in a park.
- **Flamingoes:** Horizontally pan-scanned scene of moving flamingos.
- **Buddhist images:** Vertically pan-scanned scene of Buddha statue on a cliff.
- **Driving:** High-velocity pan-scanned scene of a car going around a curve.
- **Skyscrapers:** Horizontally pan-scanned scene of buildings.
- **View from sky with credits:** Scene of river and mountains with credits scrolling vertically.

5.3   Procedure

The DSIS evaluation procedure is defined in ITU-R BT.500 and was implemented as follows.

Step 1: The sample videos were shown with the prototype system either on or off to 15 evaluators.

Step 2: Each evaluator rated the picture quality in accordance with the scale listed in Table 2.

Table 2. Level of disturbance and rating scale

Disturbance	Score
Imperceptible	5
Perceptible but not annoying	4
Slightly annoying	3
Annoying	2
Very annoying	1

Step 3: Steps 1 and 2 were done by the 15 evaluators for case (a), in which they viewed the original videos on the screen, and for case (b), in which they viewed the same videos recorded using the digital camcorders and cell phone with digital camera. For each video and for each case, the average of the 15 scores was used as the quality level. To evaluate the effect of the prototype system, the above steps were performed at five different flashing frequencies (continuous, 5, 10, 15, and 20 Hz).

(a) Swinging

(b) Flamingoes

(c) Buddhist images

(d) Driving

(e) Skyscrapers

(f) View from sky with credits

Fig. 6. Evaluated videos

5.4   Results

Case (a): viewing of original videos

This evaluation aimed to confirm whether the audience can see a movie displayed on the screen of the prototype without any visual degradation. All the evaluators rated the quality of all the sample videos as 5 ("imperceptible"), which means the noise signal was imperceptible for all the videos and at all flashing frequencies. We thus confirmed that the proposed method satisfied the relationship described in formula (4) and did not cause visual degradation that was perceivable to the naked eye.

Case (b): viewing of recorded videos

The evaluated videos were recording using two ordinary digital camcorders (1/6-inch CCD based and 1/3.2-inch CMOS based) and a cell phone with a CMOS-based digital camera. Figure 7 shows still images of the videos on the proposed screen shot using the three recorders. Figures 8 through 10 plot the evaluation results for each recorder. The horizontal axis represents the flashing frequency of the noise signal (0 Hz means continuous). The vertical axis represents the quality level, μ, which is the average of the 15 scores in the range [$\mu - \sigma$, $\mu + \sigma$], where σ is the standard deviation in quality level. The results for the two camcorders show that the 10-Hz noise signal was the most degraded and that the quality level at 10 Hz was less than 2 (annoying). The cell phone recording had the highest level of disturbance.

(1) CMOS camcorder

In all of the evaluation images shot with the CMOS camcorder, the steady noise signal had the smallest disturbance. The quality level ranged from 3.1 to 3.9 for the six images. The flashing noise signal resulted in quality levels ranging from 1.7 to 3.2, and flashing at 10 Hz yielded the biggest disturbance: the quality level was from 1.7 to 3.2. This result shows that the Bartley effect was effective. The effect of the noise signal tended to be larger for images with lower luminance values ("Swinging") and smaller for images with higher luminance values ("Skyscrapers"). The scores varied more than those for the CCD camcorder and cellular phone.

(2) CCD camcorder

The quality level for the continuous noise signal ranged from 2.6 to 3.5 for the six images, whereas the quality level for the flashing noise signal was from 1.5 to 2.0. The flashing frequency of 10 Hz was the most disturbing; the quality level ranged from 1.7 to 3.2. The quality level and variation in scores for each image showed the same trend as those for the CMOS-based camcorder.

(1) CMOS-based digital camcorder

(2) CCD-based digital camcorder

(3) Cellular phone with CMOS-based camera

Fig. 7. Images shot with three recorders

(3) Cellular phone with CMOS digital camera

The quality of all the sample videos was 2 or less for all the flashing frequencies. We attribute this to the fact that the digital cameras on cellular phones are not equipped with IR-cut filters in order to lower manufacturing costs and save weight, so they react more to noise signals. The reason the quality level for the flash frequency of 15 Hz was as high as that for the continuous noise signal is that the light was recorded as continuous light by the cellular phone camera, which has a lower frame rate than the two camcorders. The variation in the scores was the smallest and did not depend on the evaluator or video.

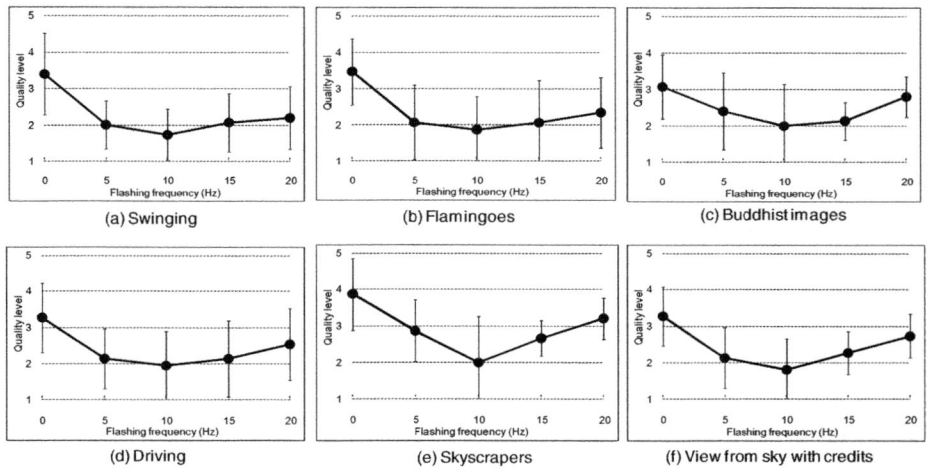

Fig. 8. Evaluation results (CMOS-based digital camcorder)

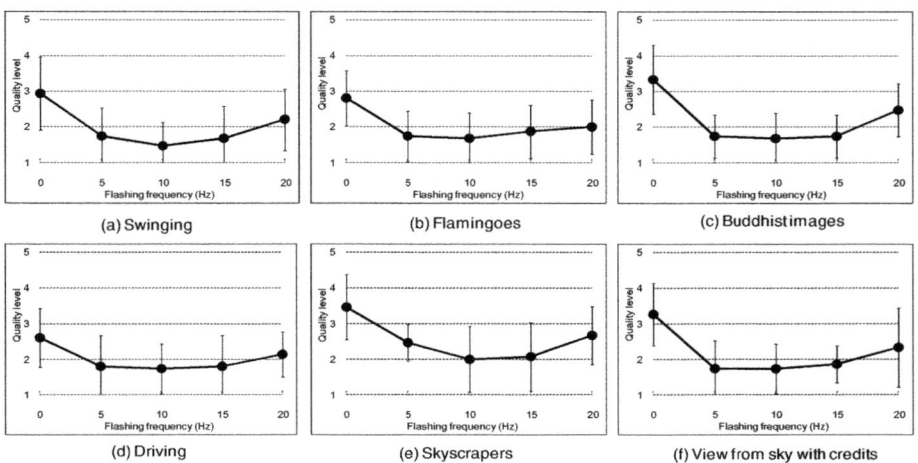

Fig. 9. Evaluation results (CCD-based digital camcorder)

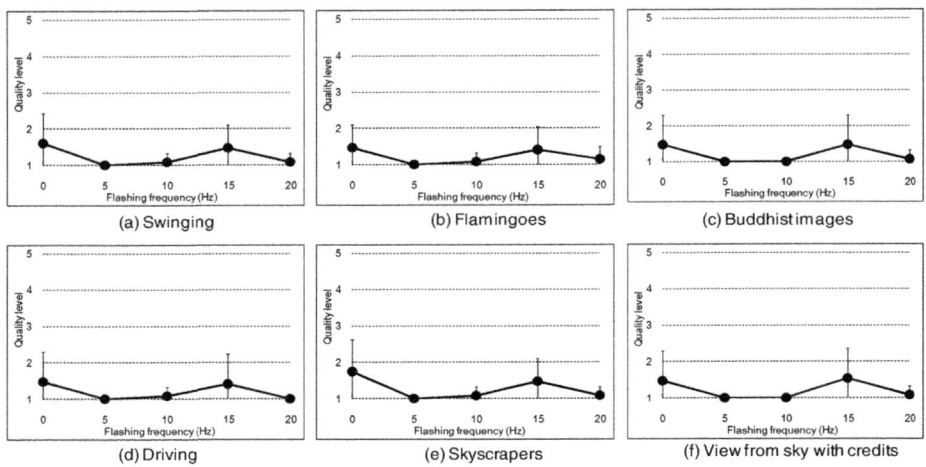

Fig. 10. Evaluation results (cellular phone with CMOS-based digital camera)

6 Countermeasure against Use of IR-Cut Filter on Camera

The method described above is ineffective against illegal recording using digital cameras and camcorders equipped with an IR-cut filter, which eliminates noise. However, there is a simple countermeasure against the use of an IR-cut filter. It is based on detecting the IR light reflected off the filter and exploiting the IR specular reflection of the filter.

6.1 Principle

Illegal recording is done by pointing the camcorder towards the screen. Therefore, an IR-cut filter attached to the lens of the camcorder would face the screen. The countermeasure we propose is to place an IR camcorder behind the screen in order to detect the specular IR light reflected by the filter.

Figure 11 illustrates the countermeasure together with the system for the illegal recording prevention described in Section 4. The proposed measure is implemented by attaching IR emission units at regular intervals behind the screen, placing an IR camcorder with a visible range cut filter behind the screen at the center to detect IR light reflected from an IR-cut filter, and running an algorithm on a PC to analyze the detected light. An IR-cut filter is a planar filter with a dielectric multilayer, and it reflects IR light from the various incoming directions in a single outgoing direction (specular reflection). The algorithm can thus detect an attack using a camcorder with an IR-cut filter by analyzing the specular reflections picked up by the IR camcorder.

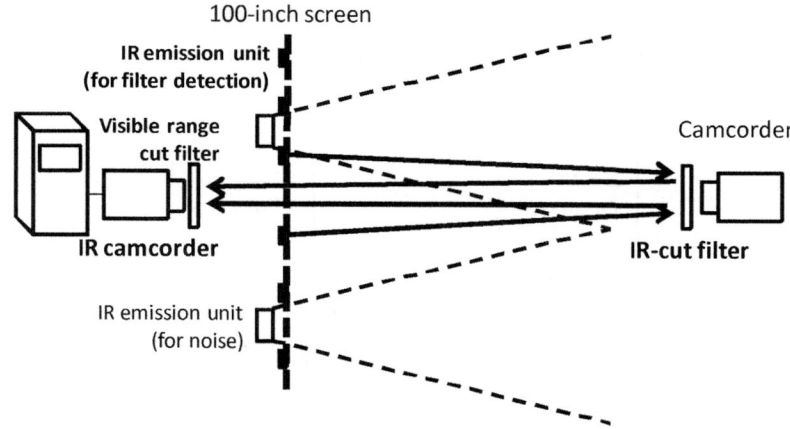

Fig. 11. Proposed countermeasure

6.2   Filter Detection Algorithm

Figure 12 shows the flowchart of the filter detection algorithm. The input is a pair of videos from the IR camcorder.

Video (a): shot in room without audience
Video (b): shot in room with audience

Video (a) is used for eliminating reflections off objects in the room that also appear in video (b). The procedure comprises eight steps.

Step 1. Input image frames of video (a) and eliminate effect of flashing (from IR emission units).

Step 2. Average processed image frames and generate one averaged image frame.

Step 3. Repeat steps 3-1 through 3-5 for each series of image frames of video (b) input from IR camcorder.

Step 3-1. Input image frames of video (b) and eliminate effect of flashing.
Step 3-2. Subtract pixel values of averaged image frame of video (a) generated in step 2 from those of each image frame of video (b) processed in step 3-1.
Step 3-3. Estimate motion areas of video (b) from image frames processed in step 3-1.
Step 3-4. Eliminate motion areas of video (b) using results of motion estimation (step 3-3) and eliminate diffuse reflection objects of video (b).
Step 3-5. Calculate areas for each reflection area, Ss, of video (b) and compare them with threshold T. Detect attack and show location of filter if area is larger than T.

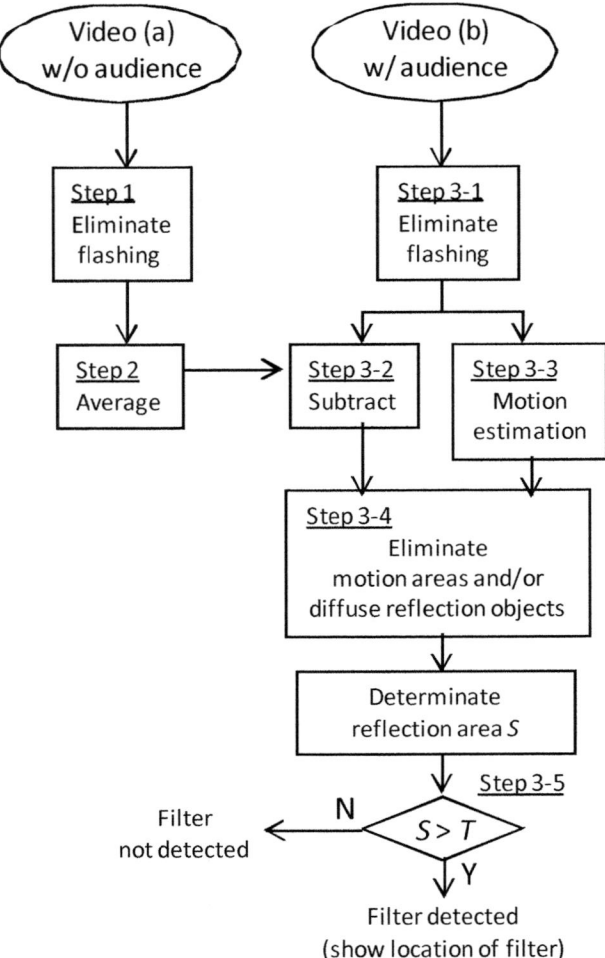

Fig. 12. Filter detection algorithm

6.3   Prototype

We implemented the countermeasure in the prototype system described in Section 4. Figure 13 shows an overview of the system. The system comprises an IR camcorder with a short-wavelength cut filter (cut-on wavelength of 870 nm), 36 IR emission units (IR LEDs with peak wavelength of 940 nm) arranged in a 6 by 6 grid for filter detection, and nine IR noise emission units (IR LEDs with peak wavelength of 870 nm and a short-wavelength cut filter (cut-on wavelength of 870 nm)).

We evaluated the ability of the system to detect an IR-cut filter. As shown in Figure 14 (a), we placed objects that would normally be in a theater at a distance of ~45 m from the screen. Figure 14 (b) shows the results of the filter detection algorithm. We set T to 10 (pixels). The area circled in red was detected by the algorithm as the location of an IR-cut filter; it corresponds to the camcorder with the filter. The proposed countermeasure is thus effective against the use of a camcorder equipped with an IR-cut filter.

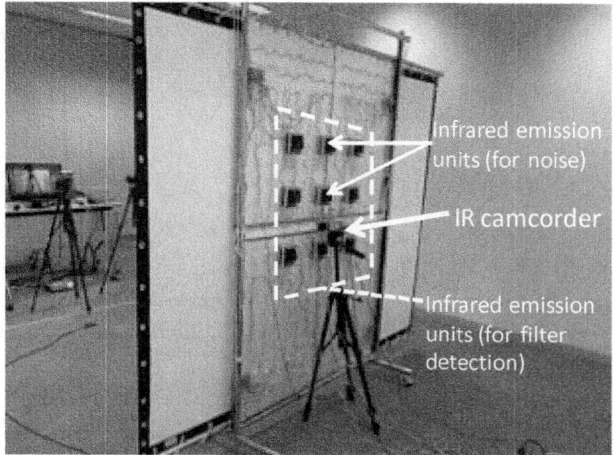

Fig. 13. System overview

7   Conclusion

Preventing the illegal recording of videos and movies is essential for enforcing copyrights. While laws against illegal recording have been passed and technologies for watermarking images have been developed, a practical method for preventing illegal recording is still needed. We have developed and tested a method that exploits the differences in sensory characteristics between humans and devices to prevent videos and movies displayed on a screen or monitor from being illegally recorded. This method uses a noise signal invisible to the human eye but can be picked up by a camcorder and does not require the addition of a function to camcorders.

The noise signal used should not degrade the movie viewed in the theatre by the audience but should maximize the noise in a recording of the movie. To this end, we use infrared LEDs equipped with a short-wavelength cut filter and flashing noise in a manner that creates the Bartley effect.

We developed a functional prototype system for illegal recording prevention, implemented it on a 100-inch cinema screen, and conducted a subjective evaluation experiment with it. The results demonstrated the validity of our method. We also devised an effective countermeasure against a simple attack wherein the recording camera is equipped with an infrared cut filter. Future work will focus on applying our method to various types of displays including LCDs and LED monitors.

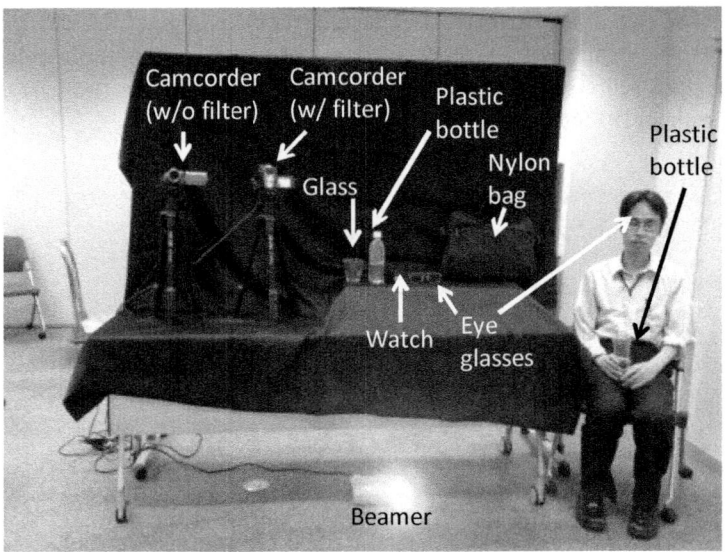

(a) Evaluated objects

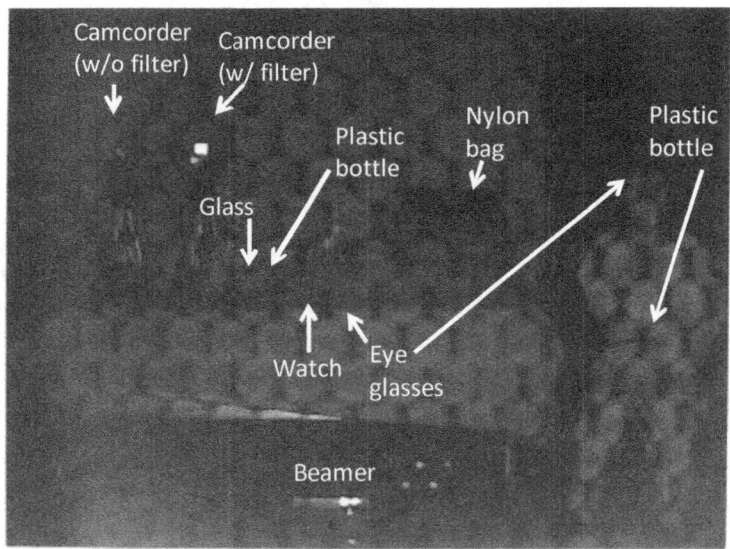

(b) Evaluation results

Fig. 14. System evaluation

References

1. The Motion Picture Association of America (MPAA), http://www.mpaa.org/
2. Ezra, E., Rowden, T. (eds.): Transnational Cinema: The Film Reader. Routledge (2006)
3. Haitsma, J., Kaler, T.: A Watermarking Scheme for Digital Cinema. In: Proc. 2001 International Conference on Image Processing (ICIP 2001), vol. 2, pp. 487–489 (2001)

4. Gohshi, S., Nakamura, H., Ito, H., Fujii, R., Suzuki, M., Takai, S., Tani, Y.: A New Watermark Surviving After Re-shooting the Images Displayed on a Screen. In: Khosla, R., Howlett, R.J., Jain, L.C. (eds.) KES 2005, Part II. LNCS (LNAI), vol. 3682, pp. 1099–1107. Springer, Heidelberg (2005)
5. Nakamura, H., Gohshi, S., Fujii, R., Ito, H., Suzuki, M., Takai, S., Tani, Y.: A Digital Watermark that Survives after Re-shooting the Images Displayed on a CRT Screen. Journal of the Institute of Image Information and Television Engineers 60(11), 1778–1788 (2006)
6. Nakashima, Y., Tachibana, R., Babaguchi, N.: Watermarked Movie Soundtrack Finds the Position of the Camcorder in Theater. IEEE Transactions on Multimedia 11(3), 443–454 (2009)
7. Lee, M., Kim, K., Lee, H.: Digital Cinema Watermarking for Estimating the Position of the Pirate. IEEE Transactions on Multimedia 12(7), 605–621 (2010)
8. Rosenblatt, B., Trippe, B., Mooney, S.: Digital Rights Management - Business and Technology. M&T Books (2003)
9. Content Scramble System (CSS), http://www.dvdcca.org/css.aspx
10. Bourdon, P., Thiebaud, S., Doyen, D.: A theoretical analysis of spatial/temporal modulation-based systems for prevention of illegal recordings in movie theaters. In: Proc. SPIE. Security, Forensics, Steganography, and Watermarking of Multimedia Contents X, vol. 6819, p. 1389 (2008)
11. Schanda, J. (ed.): Colorimetry: Understanding the CIE system. Wiley-Interscience (2007)
12. Menn, N.: Practical Optics. Academic Press (2004)
13. Gonzalez, R., Woods, R.: Digital Image Processing, 3rd edn. Prentice Hall (2007)
14. Holst, G., Lomheim, T.: CMOS/CCD Sensors and Camera Systems. SPIE-International Society for Optical Engine (2007)
15. Halstead, W.: A note on the Bartley effect in the estimation of equivalent brightness. Journal of Experimental Psychology 28(6), 524–528 (1941)
16. Rec. ITU-R BT.500-11, Methodology for the subjective assessment of the quality of television pictures (2002)
17. The Institute of Image Information and Television Engineers, Evaluation video sample (standard definition)
18. ITU Radiocommunication Sector (ITU-R),
    http://www.itu.int/ITU-R/index.asp?category=
    information&rlink=rhome&lang=en
19. ITU Telecommunication Standardization Sector (ITU-T),
    http://www.itu.int/ITU-T/index.html

Secure Watermarking on 3D Geometry via ICA and Orthogonal Transformation

Hao-tian Wu[1] and Yiu-ming Cheung[2],[*]

[1] School of Information Science and Technology
Sun Yat-Sen University, Guangzhou, China
whaot@mail.sysu.edu.cn
[2] Department of Computer Science,
Hong Kong Baptist University, Hong Kong, China
ymc@comp.hkbu.edu.hk

Abstract. The technique of independent component analysis (ICA) has been utilized in digital image and audio watermarking. In this paper, it is applied to improve the security of 3D geometry watermarking by using the ICA de-mixing matrix for transformation. An orthogonal transformation (OT) matrix is further employed so that another watermarking scheme is generated. With the same embedding method, the two watermarking schemes are implemented on the test models. The experimental results show that they have similar performance in imperceptibility and capacity. As both of them have the properties of blind extraction and security, the OT-based scheme can be regarded as a simplified version of the ICA-based one with less computational cost.

1 Introduction

In the field of digital watermarking [1,2], the technique of independent component analysis (ICA) [3,4] has been utilized for digital images (e.g. [6], [7] and [8]) and audio signals (e.g. [9,10]). ICA is a versatile technique that was initially used for blind source separation. One kind of ICA can be represented in the model $\mathbf{x} = A\mathbf{s}$, where $\mathbf{x} = [x_1, x_2, \ldots, x_n]^T$ denotes an observed vector whose element is the mixture of n independent components: $s_1, s_2, \ldots, s_n$ in the source vector $\mathbf{s}$ (also called feature vector hereinafter). A is the mixing matrix with elements a_{ij} so that $x_i = a_{i1}s_1 + a_{i2}s_2 + \ldots + a_{in}s_n$ for $i \in \{1, 2, \ldots, n\}$. Without knowing A, the purpose of ICA is to estimate $\mathbf{s}$ up to a constant scalar and any permutation of component order from the observation $\mathbf{x}$ by finding out a de-mixing matrix W so that $\mathbf{s} = W\mathbf{x}$.

In the literature, the ICA technique has been applied to digital watermarking along two different ways. One is to use the ICA de-mixing matrix for transformation to embed data in the feature space (i.e. the space of $\mathbf{s}$), such as the algorithms in [6]-[8]. The basic idea of such a method is to use the de-mixing matrix W to map $\mathbf{x}$ to the ICA feature space. Subsequently, data embedding is performed in

---

* Corresponding author.

Y.Q. Shi (Ed.): Transactions on DHMS VII, LNCS 7110, pp. 52–62, 2012.

the feature space by changing the values of the components $\mathbf{s} = \{s_1, s_2, \ldots, s_n\}$ to $\mathbf{t} = \{t_1, t_2, \ldots, t_n\}$. The watermarked signal $\mathbf{y}$ will be obtained after we transform $\mathbf{t}$ with the mixing matrix A, i.e., $\mathbf{y} = A\mathbf{t}$. To extract the embedded data, we need to transform $\mathbf{y}$ back to the ICA feature space by $\mathbf{t} = W\mathbf{y}$. Hence, the de-mixing matrix W acts as a key to both data embedding and extraction, and a new form of security is enabled by keeping the matrix W and its inverse secret. In [6], part of the independent components of the original image are replaced by those of the watermark image, similar to the least significant bits (LSB) replacement in the spatial domain. Since the replaced components are with less energy, and the components of the watermark are assigned with a weight as well, the perceptual quality of the image can be preserved. However, the data hiding capacity is low at the expense of storing two mixing matrices as the keys for the original image and the watermark, respectively. In [7], ICA has been utilized for watermarking of digital images by modulating the independent components with the Quantization Index Modulation (QIM) method [11]. By this means, high data hiding capacity is reachable, especially in the fragile watermarking scheme where a large set of components are selected. In [7], the ICA de-mixing matrix is estimated from a training set of 11 natural scene images so that it can be used for blind watermarking, i.e. extracting the embedded watermark without any information regarding to the original image. In addition, low computational cost is required by using the pre-computed matrix. The same method is also applied to the audio signals as shown in [8].

The other way of applying ICA to digital watermarking is mainly based on the idea of viewing watermark extraction as a problem of blind source separation. In [9], the key and the watermark, which are special images with the same size as the original image, are linearly mixed with the original image to generate the watermarked image. By regarding the watermarked image as an observed mixture, the watermark recovery can be viewed as a blind source separation problem and its accuracy depends on the statistical independence among the key, the watermark, and the original image. Since both the key and the original image are required for the watermark extraction, the watermarking algorithm is applicable to private applications, e.g. copyright protection, and its robustness to the attacks has been examined as well. Furthermore, the idea of viewing watermark extraction as a blind source separation problem has also been adopted for multimedia authenticity protection. In [10], a covert independent watermark signal serves as a "vaccine" against a dormant digital "bacteria" to protect the multimedia data. Once the unauthorized removal of the watermark is detected, a program is triggered to take an appropriate action, such as degrading of quality. The robustness of the ICA digital watermarking with respect to lossy compression, such as the compatibility with the popular MP3 format for digital music files, has been measured. The dynamic range of the digital watermark as clutter versus the original music, which is a signal coded under the MP3 format, has also been investigated.

In this paper, we aim to improve the security of 3D geometry watermarking by using the ICA de-mixing matrix for transformation. To make it suitable for blind watermarking and reduce the computational cost as well, the de-mixing matrix is not estimated from the original geometry, but from a set of geometries other than it. The popular FastICA algorithm [5] is employed to estimate the ICA mixing and de-mixing matrices. To make the transformation matrix independent from the host signal, a randomly generated orthogonal matrix except the identity one and its permutations is further used. Since the ICA matrix is also orthogonal after the whitening preprocessing in the estimation process, the requirement on the transformation matrix is actually relaxed. However, the watermarking scheme via orthogonal transformation (OT) shares some properties with the ICA-based one. For instance, the capacity will not be affected if the ICA de-mixing matrix is replaced by another orthogonal matrix. The dither modulation [11] is employed in both of the OT-based or ICA-based schemes to modify the vectors in the transform domain for data embedding. The two watermarking schemes are implemented on the test models, and the experimental results show that they have similar performance in imperceptibility and capacity. As both of them have good performance in security and blind extraction, the OT-based scheme can be regarded as an improved version of the ICA-based one with less computational cost.

The rest of this paper is organized as follows: In Section 2, the principles of 3D geometry watermarking using ICA and orthogonal transformation will be introduced, respectively. Then, Section 3 implements the two schemes on several VRML models with the performance comparison in terms of imperceptibility, embedding capacity, computational cost, and security. Finally, we draw the concluding remarks in Section 4.

2   Two Watermarking Schemes for 3D Geometry

In the literature, a lot of watermarking algorithms (e.g. [12]-[22]) have been proposed for 3D geometries, polygonal meshes in particular. Many transformation tools have been utilized to embed data into polygonal meshes in the transform domain. Typical methods include the construction of a set of basis functions [14] to employ the spread spectrum approach [23], multi-resolution wavelet decomposition [18], principal component analysis [19], mesh spectral decomposition [20], etc. Those algorithms try to improve the robustness of the embedded watermark, especially without the presence of the original mesh. In contrast, we aim to improve the security of 3D geometry watermarking by proposing two schemes based on ICA and orthogonal transformation, respectively.

2.1   Watermarking Scheme on 3D Geometry Using ICA

Although the ICA-based scheme has been applied to digital images and audio signals, how to apply it to 3D geometry has not been addressed yet. Given

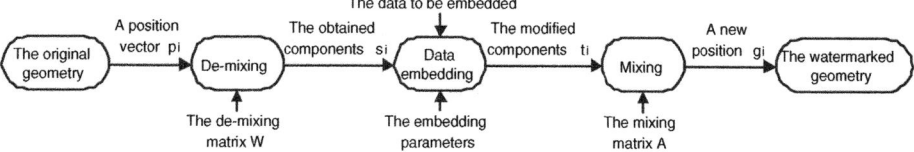

Fig. 1. The procedure of the proposed watermarking scheme for 3D geometry using independent component analysis

a 3D geometry consisting of N position vectors, the geometry can be represented by $\mathbf{P} = \{\mathbf{p_1}, \ldots, \mathbf{p_N}\}$, where a position vector $\mathbf{p_i}$ specifies the coordinates $\{p_{ix}, p_{iy}, p_{iz}\}$ in the 3D space R^3 for $i = 1, 2, \ldots, N$. For a position vector $\mathbf{p_i} = (p_{ix}, p_{iy}, p_{iz})^T$, it can be regarded as a linear combination of three statistically independent sources $\mathbf{s_i} = (s_{i1}, s_{i2}, s_{i3})^T$, i.e.

$$\mathbf{p_i} = \begin{pmatrix} p_{ix} \\ p_{iy} \\ p_{iz} \end{pmatrix} = A \times \mathbf{s_i} = \begin{pmatrix} a_{11} & a_{12} & a_{13} \\ a_{21} & a_{22} & a_{23} \\ a_{31} & a_{32} & a_{33} \end{pmatrix} \times \begin{pmatrix} s_{i1} \\ s_{i2} \\ s_{i3} \end{pmatrix}. \tag{1}$$

By using the ICA algorithm such as FastICA, we can estimate the mixing matrix A and its inverse, i.e. the de-mixing matrix W, from a set of the chosen geometries. If we directly estimate A from the set of position vectors $\mathbf{P}$ in the original geometry, the obtained matrix will be dependent on the original geometry so that the de-mixing matrix W estimated from each geometry is different. As a result, the data extraction will be non-blind, i.e. dependent on the original geometry. To suit for the blind watermarking applications, the de-mixing matrix W should be estimated from a set of geometries other than the original one. In this way, low computational cost is required because the only operation to be carried out for transformation is a simple matrix multiplication. With the de-mixing matrix W, every position vector can be transformed to the independent components by $\mathbf{s_i} = W\mathbf{p_i}$, i.e.

$$\mathbf{s_i} = \begin{pmatrix} s_{i1} \\ s_{i2} \\ s_{i3} \end{pmatrix} = W \times \mathbf{p_i} = A^{-1} \times \begin{pmatrix} p_{ix} \\ p_{ix} \\ p_{iy} \end{pmatrix}. \tag{2}$$

Although the obtained components $\mathbf{s_1}, \mathbf{s_2}, \ldots, \mathbf{s_N}$ are not as independent from each other as possible because the de-mixing matrix W is estimated from a set of geometries instead of the original one, the advantage is the blind watermarking of 3D geometry with less computational cost.

Data embedding can be performed in the ICA feature space by changing the component vector $\mathbf{s_i}$ to a new one $\mathbf{t_i} = (t_{i1}, t_{i2}, t_{i3})^T$. The position vector $\mathbf{g_i}$ in the watermarked geometry can be generated by

$$\mathbf{g_i} = \begin{pmatrix} g_{ix} \\ g_{iy} \\ g_{iz} \end{pmatrix} = A \times \mathbf{t_i} = \begin{pmatrix} a_{11} & a_{12} & a_{13} \\ a_{21} & a_{22} & a_{23} \\ a_{31} & a_{32} & a_{33} \end{pmatrix} \times \begin{pmatrix} t_{i1} \\ t_{i2} \\ t_{i3} \end{pmatrix}. \tag{3}$$

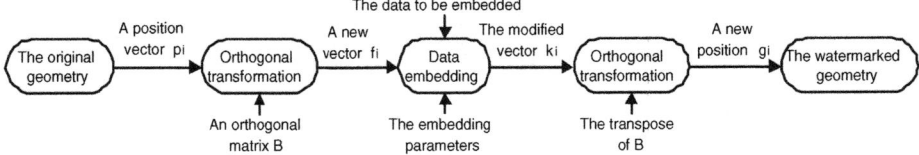

Fig. 2. The procedure of watermarking scheme for 3D geometry via orthogonal transformation

The whole watermarked geometry $\mathbf{G} = \{\mathbf{g_1}, \ldots, \mathbf{g_N}\}$ will be formed after every position vector in it has been generated. The watermarking scheme for 3D geometry using ICA is illustrated in Fig. 1, with the ICA de-mixing matrix W estimated from a set of geometries other than the original one.

Dither modulation [11] is employed to modify each element in the component vector $\mathbf{s_i}$ for data embedding. In total, a string of $3N$ bit values are embedded. To extract the embedded data from $\mathbf{G} = \{\mathbf{g_1}, \mathbf{g_2}, \ldots, \mathbf{g_N}\}$ in the watermarked geometry, we need to transform $\mathbf{G}$ with W to generate every vector within the set of modified components $\{\mathbf{t_1}, \mathbf{t_2}, \ldots, \mathbf{t_N}\}$, respectively. With the parameters used in the embedding process, data extraction can be performed from each element in the set of $\{\mathbf{t_1}, \mathbf{t_2}, \ldots, \mathbf{t_N}\}$.

2.2 Watermarking Scheme on 3D Geometry via Orthogonal Transformation

In the ICA-based data hiding scheme, the de-mixing matrix W is estimated from a set of the chosen geometries to transform the original geometry to the ICA feature space. Here, we relax the requirement by performing the transformation with an orthogonal matrix independent from 3D geometry. As a result, the generation of the transformation matrix is significantly simplified while the new scheme is suitable for blind watermarking of 3D geometry. For an orthogonal matrix Q, its transpose Q^T is just its inverse:

$$QQ^T = I, \tag{4}$$

where I is the identity matrix. An orthogonal matrix Q corresponds to an orthogonal transformation, which is a linear transformation that preserves the inner product of any two vectors in the Euclidean space R^n.

Orthogonal transformation of 3D geometry is performed by multiplying every vector $\mathbf{p_i}$ with a 3×3 orthogonal matrix B so that a new vector $\mathbf{f_i} = (f_{ix}, f_{iy}, f_{iz})^T$ in R^3 is obtained by

$$\mathbf{f_i} = \begin{pmatrix} f_{ix} \\ f_{iy} \\ f_{iz} \end{pmatrix} = B \times \mathbf{p_i} = \begin{pmatrix} b_{11} & b_{12} & b_{13} \\ b_{21} & b_{22} & b_{23} \\ b_{31} & b_{32} & b_{33} \end{pmatrix} \times \begin{pmatrix} p_{ix} \\ p_{iy} \\ p_{iz} \end{pmatrix}. \tag{5}$$

Table 1. The VRML models used in the experiments

Model	Vertices	Polygons	Capacity(bits)
lamp	676	1288	2028
pear	891	1704	2673
sgilogo	1224	1620	3672
indigo	8389	10187	25167
gears	24546	8182	73638

As there is no difference before and after the transformation if the identity matrix is used, the identity matrix and its permutations should be avoided in choosing B. Data embedding is performed in the transform domain by changing $\mathbf{f_i}$ to $\mathbf{k_i} = (k_{ix}, k_{iy}, k_{iz})^T$ for $i = 1, 2, \ldots, N$. The watermarked geometry can be therefore obtained by multiplying $\mathbf{k_i}$ with B^T so that a new set of position vectors $\mathbf{G} = \{\mathbf{g_1}, \ldots, \mathbf{g_N}\}$ are generated, respectively, by

$$\mathbf{g_i} = \begin{pmatrix} g_{ix} \\ g_{iy} \\ g_{iz} \end{pmatrix} = B^T \times \mathbf{k_i} = \begin{pmatrix} b_{11} & b_{21} & b_{31} \\ b_{12} & b_{22} & b_{32} \\ b_{13} & b_{23} & b_{33} \end{pmatrix} \times \begin{pmatrix} k_{ix} \\ k_{iy} \\ k_{iz} \end{pmatrix}. \tag{6}$$

The aforementioned scheme for 3D geometry via orthogonal transformation is illustrated in Fig. 2. Similar to the ICA-based scheme in Section 2.1, dither modulation is employed to modify each element in the set of vectors $\{\mathbf{f_1}, \ldots, \mathbf{f_N}\}$ to embed a string of $3N$ bit values with a secret key. To extract the embedded data, the position vectors $\mathbf{G} = \{\mathbf{g_1}, \mathbf{g_2}, \ldots, \mathbf{g_N}\}$ in the watermarked geometry should be transformed with B to produce every vector in the set of $\{\mathbf{k_1}, \mathbf{k_2}, \ldots, \mathbf{k_N}\}$, respectively. With the parameters used in the embedding and secret key, data extraction can be performed in the transform domain.

Suppose $\mathbf{k_i} = \mathbf{f_i} + \delta_\mathbf{i}$, where $\delta_\mathbf{i} = (\delta_{ix}, \delta_{iy}, \delta_{iz})^T$ is the change of $\mathbf{f_i}$ caused by data embedding. It can be seen that the difference between $\mathbf{g_i}$ and $\mathbf{p_i}$ is $B^T \delta_\mathbf{i}$. Since B^T is also an orthogonal matrix, the length of $B^T \delta_\mathbf{i}$ is always equal to that of $\delta_\mathbf{i}$, as denoted by

$$|B^T \delta_\mathbf{i}| = |\delta_\mathbf{i}|. \tag{7}$$

Note that an orthogonal transformation is a linear transformation that preserves the inner product of two vectors. In particular, both the lengths of the vectors and the angles between them are preserved by orthogonal transformation so that the shape of 3D geometry is preserved as well. Therefore, the distortion of 3D shape caused by data embedding in the transform domain is exactly that in the spatial domain. In other words, the distortion introduced to 3D geometry in the OT-based data hiding scheme can be directly controlled in the transform domain. In other words, there is little mutual information between the watermarked geometry and the orthogonal transformation matrix.

3   Performance Analysis and Comparison

The ICA-based and OT-based schemes were implemented on several VRML models listed in Table I, where the corresponding embedding capacities are given. A string of binary numbers were randomly generated as the watermark. In the OT-based scheme, an orthogonal matrix B was randomly generated, avoiding the identity matrix and its permutations. As for the ICA-based scheme, the de-mixing matrix W was estimated from a set of geometries other than the original one. In both of the two schemes, a dither sequence was generated by using a secret key as the seed of pseudo-random number generator. By setting the quantization step-size $\Delta = 0.000005$ and choosing the dither sequence within the interval of $(-\frac{\Delta}{2}, \frac{\Delta}{2})$, the pictures rendered from the original and watermarked mesh models of "sgilogo" and "gears" using the OT-based scheme are shown in Fig. 3.

3.1   Imperceptibility

To measure the geometrical distortion of the mesh content, the 3D signal-to-noise ratio (3D SNR) is defined as follows: Given N vertices in a 3D mesh model, the vertex positions in the original mesh are represented by $\mathbf{P} = \{\mathbf{p_1}, \ldots, \mathbf{p_N}\}$, while the vertex positions in the watermarked mesh are denoted as $\mathbf{G} = \{\mathbf{g_1}, \ldots, \mathbf{g_N}\}$. By using the mean square function $MS(\cdot)$, the 3D SNR is defined by

$$SNR = 10 \log_{10} \frac{MS(\mathbf{P} - \overline{\mathbf{P}})}{MS(\mathbf{G} - \mathbf{P})}, \tag{8}$$

where $\overline{\mathbf{P}} = \{\overline{p}_x, \overline{p}_y, \overline{p}_z\}$ is the mean of $\mathbf{P}$, and

$$\begin{cases} MS(\mathbf{P} - \overline{\mathbf{P}}) = \frac{\sum_{i=1}^{N} (p_{ix} - \overline{p}_x)^2 + (p_{iy} - \overline{p}_y)^2 + (p_{iz} - \overline{p}_z)^2}{N} \\ MS(\mathbf{G} - \mathbf{P}) = \frac{\sum_{i=1}^{N} (g_{ix} - p_{ix})^2 + (g_{iy} - p_{iy})^2 + (g_{iz} - p_{iz})^2}{N} \end{cases} . \tag{9}$$

Here $\mathbf{P} - \overline{\mathbf{P}}$ represents the signal, and $\mathbf{G} - \mathbf{P} = \mathbf{G} - \overline{\mathbf{P}} - (\mathbf{P} - \overline{\mathbf{P}})$ is the noise.

In the experiments, the impact of data embedding could be tuned by the quantization step-size Δ. In the OT-based scheme, if 0.0001 and 0.00001 were assigned to Δ, the obtained 3D SNRs of the watermarked geometry "pear" were about 52.78 and 72.60, respectively. As shown in Fig. 4 (a), the 3D SNR of the watermarked geometry decreases if the quantization step-size Δ is increased. The difference between the 3D SNR values of the watermarked geometry generated by the OT-based and ICA-based schemes is shown in Fig. 4 (b). It can be seen from Fig. 4 that the distortion of the watermarked geometry in the OT-based and ICA-based schemes is close, for the difference between the 3D SNR values of the watermarked geometry is relatively small and fluctuates around zero.

3.2   Embedding Capacity

Given N position vectors in a 3D geometry, such as N vertices in a polygonal mesh or N points in a point cloud, the embedding capacities by using the OT-based and ICA-based watermarking schemes are both $3N$ bits, as three bit values

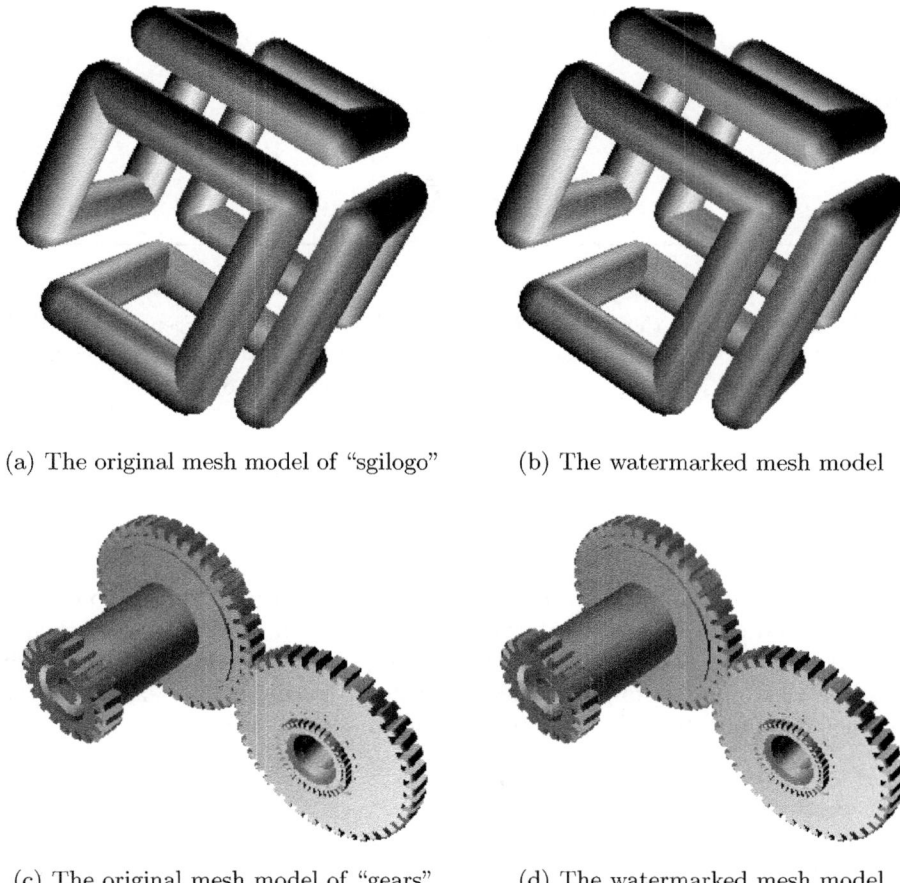

(a) The original mesh model of "sgilogo"   (b) The watermarked mesh model

(c) The original mesh model of "gears"   (d) The watermarked mesh model

Fig. 3. The original mesh models, the watermarked ones generated by setting the quantization step-size $\Delta = 0.000005$ and the dither sequence within $(-\frac{\Delta}{2}, \frac{\Delta}{2})$ in the OT-based data hiding scheme, respectively

can be embedded in a 3D vector. The embedding capacity with any scheme is higher than the existing algorithms, such as $3N - 2$ bits in [17] and $N - 1$ bits in [22]. Different from [17], the upper bound of capacity is achievable for any 3D geometry, despite whether it is a manifold triangle mesh or not.

3.3 Computational Cost and Blind Extraction

Compared with estimating the ICA de-mixing matrix from a set of 3D geometries, it is much simpler to randomly generate an orthogonal matrix for transformation. So the OT-based scheme has less computational cost than the ICA-based one. In the OT-based scheme, the randomly generated orthogonal matrix is independent from the original geometry so that it can be used for any geometry. In

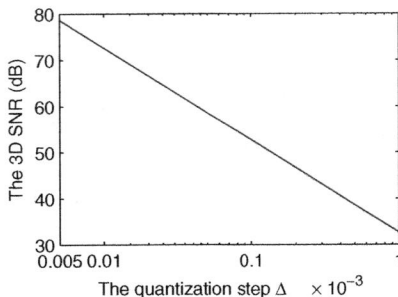
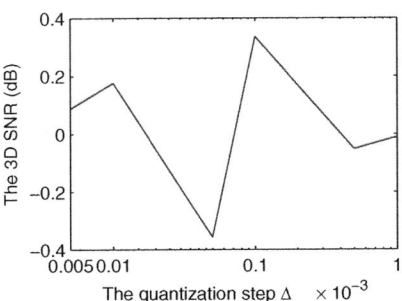

(a) 3D SNR value of the watermarked geometry "pear" generated by using the OT-based scheme

(b) The difference between the 3D SNR values of the watermarked geometry "pear" generated by the OT-based and ICA-based schemes, respectively

Fig. 4. The distortion of the VRML geometry "pear" introduced by the OT-based and ICA-based watermarking schemes varies with the quantization step-size Δ used

addition, no information regarding the original geometry is required to extract the embedded data from the watermarked geometry. In the ICA-based scheme, the ICA de-mixing matrix can also be used for blind extraction applications if it is estimated from a set of geometries other than the original one, although the obtained components will not be as independent as possible.

3.4   Security

The OT-based and ICA-based watermarking schemes share the following properties: (1) By transforming 3D coordinates with an invertible matrix, it is hard for an opponent to access the transform domain by keeping the transformation matrix secret. In the experiments, the extracted values were quite different from the embedded ones when the extraction process was not performed in the transform domain. (2) By using the technique of dither modulation, it is hard to estimate the quantization step-size Δ from the watermarked geometry. It is hard for an opponent to estimate the transformation matrix because there is little mutual information between it and the watermarked geometry. Therefore, it is even harder for an opponent to extract the data hidden in the watermarked geometry without knowing the quantization step-size Δ and dither sequence used in the embedding process.

The difference between the OT-based and ICA-based schemes lies in the generation of the transformation matrix. In the OT-based scheme, the orthogonal matrix is randomly generated so that it is independent from the 3D geometry. As for the ICA-based scheme, it is also hard to infer the ICA de-mixing matrix, which is estimated from a set of geometries other than the original one, from the watermarked geometry. Therefore, the transformation matrix randomly generated in the OT-based scheme is more secure.

4   Concluding Remarks

In this paper, the technique of ICA has been applied to 3D geometry watermarking by transforming the position vectors with the ICA de-mixing matrix. The requirement on the transformation matrix has been relaxed by using a randomly generated orthogonal matrix instead of the ICA de-mixing one. Thus, 3D geometry watermarking can be performed based on orthogonal transformation (OT). The two proposed schemes have been implemented on several VRML models by modulating the vectors in the transform domain. The numerical results have shown that the OT-based watermarking scheme is more suitable for blind watermarking of 3D geometry than the ICA-based one. By using the OT-based scheme, it is hard for an opponent to estimate the transformation matrix used for embedding or extract the data embedded in the watermarked geometry illegally.

Acknowledgment. This work was supported by NSFC (No.61100169), the Fundamental Research Funds for the Central Universities in China (No.09lgpy61), and the Research Grant Council of Hong Kong SAR under Grant No. HKBU 2156/04E and HKBU 210309. The VRML models used in the experiments are downloaded from http://www.martinreddy.net/ukvrsig/vrml.html

References

1. Cox, I.J., Miller, M.L., Bloom, J.A.: Digital Watermarking. Morgan Kaufmann, New York (2001)
2. Katzenbeisser, S., Petitcolas, F.A.P.: Information Hiding Techniques for Steganography and Digital Watermarking. Artech House (2000)
3. Comon, P.: Independent Component Analysis - A New Concept? Signal Processing 36(3), 287–314 (1994)
4. Hyvarinen, A., Oja, E.: Independent Component Analysis: Algorithms and Applications. Neural Networks 13(4-5), 411–430 (2000)
5. Hyvarinen, A., Oja, E.: A Fast Fixed-Point Algorithm for Independent Component Analysis. Neural Computation 9(7), 1483–1492 (1997)
6. González-Serrano, F.J., Molina-Bulla, H.Y., Murillo-Fuentes, J.J.: Independent Component Analysis Applied to Digital Watermarking. In: International Conference on Acoustic, Speech and Signal Processing (ICASSP), vol. 3, pp. 1997–2000 (2001)
7. Bounkong, S., Toch, B., Saad, D., Lowe, D.: ICA for Watermarking Digital Images. Journal of Machine Learning Research 4(7-8), 1471–1498 (2003)
8. Toch, B., Lowe, D., Saad, D.: Watermarking of Audio Signals Using Independent Component Analysis. In: Proceeding of the 3th International Conference on WEB Delivering of Music, pp. 71–74 (2003)
9. Yu, D., Sattar, F., Ma, K.-K.: Watermark Detection and Extraction Using Independent Component Analysis Method. EURASIP Journal on Applied Signal Processing 2002(1), 92–104, doi:10.1155/S111086570200046X
10. Szu, H., Noel, S., Yim, S.-B., Willey, J., Landa, J.: Multimedia Authenticity Protection with ICA Watermarking and Digital Bacteria Vaccination. Neural Networks, Special Issue for International Joint Conference on Neural Networks 16(5-6), 907–914 (2003)

11. Chen, B., Wornell, G.W.: Quantization Index Modulation: A Class of Provably Good Methods for Digital Watermarking and Information Embedding. IEEE Transactions on Information Theory 47(4), 1423–1443 (2001)
12. Ohbuchi, R., Masuda, H., Aono, M.: Watermarking Three-Dimensional Polygonal Models Through Geometric and Topological Modifications. IEEE Journal of Selected Areas in Communications 16(4), 551–560 (1998)
13. Benedens, O.: Geometry-Based Watermarking of 3-D Models. IEEE Computer Graphics and Application, Special Issue on Image Security 19(1), 46–55 (1999)
14. Praun, E., Hoppe, H., Finkelstein, A.: Robust Mesh Watermarking. In: Proceedings of ACM SIGGRAPH, pp. 69–76 (1999)
15. Yeo, B.L., Yeung, M.M.: Watermarking 3-D Objects for Verification. IEEE Computer Graphics and Application 19(1), 36–45 (1999)
16. Cayre, F., Macq, B.: Data Hiding on 3-D Triangle Meshes. IEEE Transactions on Signal Processing 51(4), 939–949 (2003)
17. Cayre, F., Devillers, O., Schmitt, F., Maitre, H.: Watermarking 3D Triangle Meshes for Authentication and Integrity. INRIA Research Report RR-5223 (2004)
18. Uccheddu, F., Corsini, M., Barni, M.: Wavelet-Based Blind Watermarking of 3d Models. In: Proceedings of ACM Multimedia & Security Workshop, Magdeburg, Germany, pp. 143–154 (2004)
19. Zafeiriou, S., Tefas, A., Pitas, I.: Blind Robust Watermarking Schemes for Copyright Protection of 3D Mesh Objects. IEEE Transactions on Visualization and Computer Graphics 11(5), 596–607 (2005)
20. Ohbuchi, R., Mukaiyama, A., Takahashi, S.: A Frequency Domain Approach to Watermarking 3D Shapes. Computer Graphics Forum 21(3), 373–382 (2002)
21. Bors, A.G.: Watermarking Mesh-Based Representations of 3-D Objects Using Local Moments. IEEE Transactions on Image Processing 15(3), 687–701 (2006)
22. Wu, H.T., Cheung, Y.M.: A High-Capacity Data Hiding Method for Polygonal Meshes. In: Camenisch, J.L., Collberg, C.S., Johnson, N.F., Sallee, P. (eds.) IH 2006. LNCS, vol. 4437, pp. 188–200. Springer, Heidelberg (2007)
23. Cox, I.J., Killian, J., Leighton, T., Shamoon, T.: Secure Spread Spectrum Watermarking for Multimedia. IEEE Transactions on Image Processing 6(12), 1673–1687 (1997)

Measuring the Statistical Correlation Inconsistencies in Mobile Images for Tamper Detection

Hong Cao[1,2] and Alex C. Kot[2]

[1] Institute for Infocomm Research, Agency for Science, Technology and Research (A*STAR),
Singapore 138632
hcao@i2r.a-star.edu.sg
[2] School of Electrical and Electronic Engineering, Nanyang Technological University,
Singapore 639798
caoh0002@e.ntu.edu.sg, eackot@ntu.edu.sg

Abstract. In this paper, we propose a novel framework to statistically measure the correlation inconsistency in mobile images for tamper detection. By first sampling a number of blocks at different image locations, we extract a set of derivative weights as features from each block using partial derivative correlation models. Through regularizing the within-image covariance eigenspectrum and performing eigenfeature transformation, we derive a compact set of eigen weights, which are sensitive to image signal mixing from different source models. A metric is then proposed to quantify the inconsistency among the sampled blocks at different image locations. Through comparison, our eigen weights features show better performance than the eigenfeatures from several other types of forensics features in detecting the presence of tampering. Experimentally, our method shows good tamper detection performance especially when a small percentage of sampled blocks are from a different camera model or brand with different demosaicing processing.

Keywords: CFA, demosaicing, forensics, image inconsistency, mobile cameras, regularity, source identification, tamper detection.

1   Introduction

Mobile images are digital color images acquired by the low-end mobile cameras attached on handheld devices, e.g. personal digital assistants and cellular phones. Fast growth of mobile devices and the popularity of incorporating cameras into these devices have made mobile images become a main stream [1]. Similar to the images acquired by digital still cameras (DSC), these low-quality mobile images can also be used as evidences of real happenings in a wide array of applications ranging from police investigation, legal service, citizen journalism [2], insurance claims to consumer photography. As the mobile images are also subject to easy manipulation, their credibility cannot be taken for granted especially in occasions where security is needed. Forensics analysis that can tell their integrity is in urgent needs.

A large number of image forensic works [4-27] have been proposed in recent years, which identify image sources, expose forgeries or both through detecting some

Y.Q. Shi (Ed.): Transactions on DHMS VII, LNCS 7110, pp. 63–81, 2012.

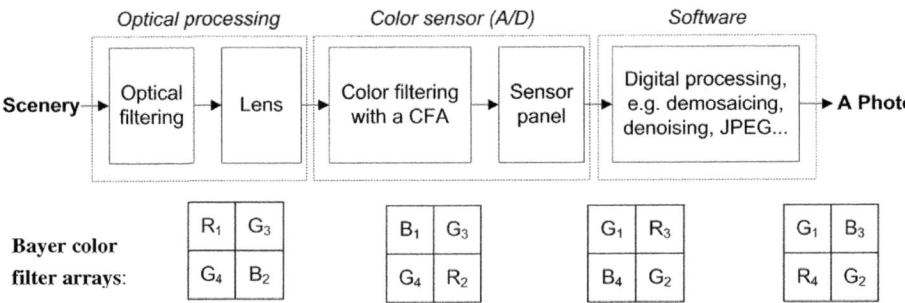

Fig. 1. Mobile camera processing pipeline and Bayer color filter array (CFA) patterns

intrinsic image regularities or some common tampering anomalies. Many different forms of image regularities and anomalies have been detected in the prior works. One can refer to [20] for the different forensics methodologies and [27] for a comprehensive bibliography. Among these tamper forensics works, Swaminathan *et al.* [6] extended their early work [4] on estimation of the color interpolation coefficients (CIC) for nonintrusive component analysis. By formulating the image manipulation as a linear time invariant filtering process, the filter parameters are estimated by a recursive deconvolution technique for detecting different forms of image manipulations. Chen *et al.* [11] improved the pixel response non-uniformity (PRNU) sensor noise model, the preprocessing techniques as well as the PRNU estimation framework to identify individual cameras and to detect integrity tampering. Avcibas *et al.* [16] proposed a method to measure image distortions in a way that is less affected by diverse image content. These distortions can be used as features for detecting some specific manipulations. Bayram *et al.* [17] combined three types of forensics features including image quality metrics (IQM), binary similarity (BS) and multi-scale wavelet statistics (MSWS) for detecting some common image manipulations. Ng *et al.* [18] and Chen *et al.* [23] proposed several statistical features to detect the presence of sharp image discontinuities caused by the splicing forgery. Johnson *et al.* [19] developed a tool to estimate the lighting direction from a point light source, where the inconsistent lighting directions can be used as an indication of tampering. He *et al.* [21] proposed to recompress a JPEG image with a high quality factor and identify the blocks that do not exhibit double-quantization effect as doctored blocks. Through analyzing the DCT coefficients, the probability for each block being doctored is estimated and the probability map helps a forensics analyst to visually identify the tampered image region. Fu *et al.* [22] discovered that the first digits of JPEG DCT coefficients closely follow a generalized Benford's law but not for the double JPEG compressed images. The violation of the generalized Benford's law is detected as an evidence of possible image tampering. Luo *et al.* [24] and Barni *et al.* [25] measured the JPEG blocking artifacts for differentiating double-compressed and single-compressed image blocks.

Though some convincing results have demonstrated for each of the above methods, the limitations shall not be overlooked in a practical scenario. Some methods either require knowledge of the tampering operations [16] or report less satisfactory results in a blind context [17]. Other methods require the source information, e.g. the ground-truth color interpolation coefficients for [6] or PRNU for [11], or they require a good number of genuine training images from the same source [11, 17]. The splicing detection methods [18, 23] would face difficulties if the splicing boundary is deliberately rendered smooth. For [19], estimation of the lighting directions on noisy image data by itself can be challenging and error prone. The methods [21, 22, 24, 25] based on detecting double JPEG quantization generally do not work for non-JPEG compressed images and some heavily JPEG compressed images. Moreover, these works are commonly evaluated on the high-quality DSC images, but not on the low-end mobile images. It is worth to note that a mobile camera is typically ten times cheaper, ten times smaller in physical size and consume ten times less power [1] than a DSC. The large amount of sensor noises due to the small sensor size would require denoising technique being implemented in the software unit. The low power consumption would require simple digital processing algorithms, where low complexity is one primary concern. The small storage space also requires smaller image file size, hence a higher default JPEG compression rate. Since these low-end software processes could render some high-frequency forensics evidences undetectable, not all forensics techniques for DSC images can be readily extended to mobile images.

For mobile images, the existing forensics works are mainly related with image source identification. Such works includes: Extending from Lucas *et al.* [10], Alles *et al.* [12] estimated PRNU patterns to identify individual mobile cameras and webcams. McKay *et al.* [5] computed both the CIC features in [4] and some noise statistics features (NStats) feature to identify different types of image acquisition devices including DSCs, mobile cameras, scanners and computer graphics. Celiktutan *et al.* [15] compared various fusion methods to combine three sets of forensics features including IQM, MSWS and BS features to distinguish various cell-phone models. Our previous work in [9] proposed to combine three sets of accurately detected demosaicing features, including weights, error cumulants and normalized group sizes [8]. Through feature reduction, our compact set of eigen features show better source identification performance than other forensics features as suggested in [5, 15]. Encouraged by the good source identification results, we extend our detection model and weights features to address the tamper forensics challenges on mobile images.

We propose to measure the correlation inconsistency from the blocks sampled at different image locations. Fig. 2 shows the flowchart of our proposed method. By first sampling a number of blocks from a mobile image, we estimate the underlying demosaicing formulas for the different demosaicing categories in terms of derivative weights. By computing the within-image covariance matrix from a representative set of training mobile images and through regularizing its eigen spectrum, we learn an eigenfeature transformation to derive a compact set of eigen weights features. These features are the most sensitive to the tampering inconsistencies as the eigenfeature transformation is learned based maximizing the between-image covariance and minimizing the within-image covariance. Since the local image tampering would likely have uneven impacts on our sampled blocks at different locations, we propose a metric to quantify this inconsistency by measuring the total variances of our derived eigen weights associated with the different sampled blocks. A tamper detection decision is then made by comparing the measured inconsistency with a decision threshold, which can be predetermined based on training statistics.

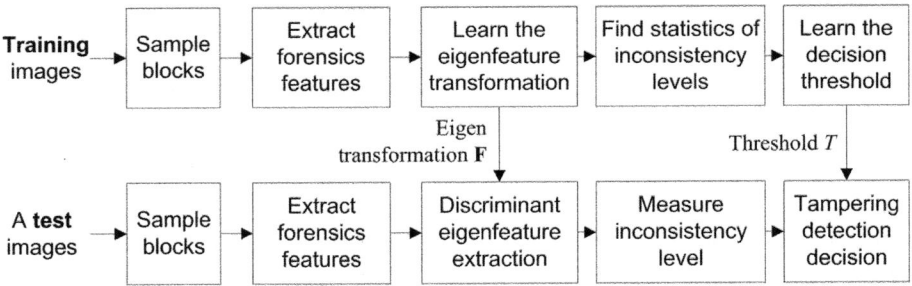

Fig. 2. Flowchart of the proposed method

Our proposed method is novel offering several contributions. First, no prior information is required about the specific image source or the specific tampering type for the test mobile image to be known in advance. The eigenfeature transformation can be learned offline based on a representative mobile image dataset from multiple sources, where the test source may not be available. Second, in learning the eigenfeature transformation, our concept of minimizing the "within-image" covariance is novel. Third, we propose a novel metric to quantify the amount of inconsistency among the image blocks sampled from different image locations. Experimentally, we show that this metric works well in detecting integrity tampering especially when image signals are mixed from different source mobile camera models or brands. Fourth, a comparison shows that our eigen weights tend to perform better than the eigen features extracted from several other types of mobile-image forensics features in detecting the tampering inconsistencies. Fifth, a sensitivity analysis is provided to investigate our tamper detection performance based on different sampling block sizes, different percentages of tampered blocks, etc.

The organization for the remainder of this paper is as follows. Section 2 details the proposed method. Section 3 experimentally shows the effectiveness and sensitivity of our proposed method in detecting the presence of tampering. Section 4 concludes this paper and discusses several possible future extensions.

2   Proposed Method

Our method in Fig. 2 quantifies the statistical correlation inconsistency based on accurately detected demosaicing weight features. Our aim is to address one most frequently asked forensics question, i.e. "Is a given digital image the original output of a camera device or has its integrity been tampered?". The idea is based on the fact that an intact mobile image often possesses good statistical harmony since different image regions has gone through the same processing pipeline as illustrated in Fig. 1(a). On another hand, tampering often involves mixing image signals from multiple sources, applying location-dependant tampering processing, or both. These would inevitably introduce some statistical inconsistencies between the intact image region and the tampered region. In the following section, we elaborate on our main steps in Fig. 2.

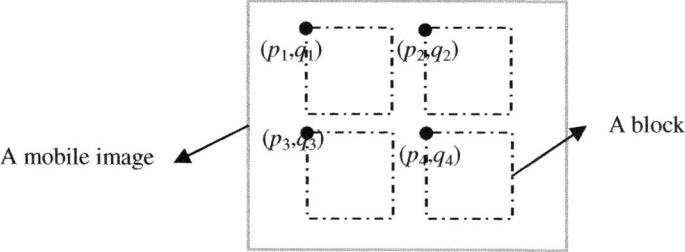

Fig. 3. Sampling blocks at different regions of a mobile image, where top-left corners (p_i, q_i) for blocks $1 \leq i \leq 4$ are set to be odd numbers to avoid shifts of the underlying CFA

2.1 Block Sampling

Many ways are available to sample some image blocks in different regions of a test mobile image. For instance, one can choose the number of blocks needed, the block size as well as the sampling locations. Several important assumptions in this sampling are: 1) the blocks should be of sufficiently large sizes so that sufficient color samples are present to ensure good estimation of the underlying forensics statistics; 2) The sampled blocks shall cover the region of interests where local tampering more likely occurs; 3) Preferably, the sampling locations can be dispersedly distributed so that some blocks fall into the intact image region and others are affected by the tampering; 4) To avoid redundancy, blocks sampled at different regions shall not overlap in a large percentage of the total block area. Since designing the sampling scheme by itself can be a separate topic, which is not the primary concern of this paper, we have adopted a simple scheme as illustrated in Fig. 3. In this scheme, four non-overlapping blocks of about 512×512 are sampled at fixed locations, which are close to image center. For a typical 3 to 5 megapixel mobile image, these four blocks would be able to cover the central image area, which is often the region of interest. The image coordinates (p_i, q_i) of the top-left corner of the *ith* sample box are set to be odd numbers. Because we are using derivative weights as features in this paper, this is to ensure that we do not artificially create an unnecessary shift of the underlying CFA patterns for the sampled blocks at different locations. Our previous research [8] has shown that derivative weights estimated based on the four different shifted versions of Bayer CFAs in Fig. 1 are usually distinctively different.

2.2 Estimation of Derivative Weights

We estimate the derivative correlation weights for a sampled block **P** based on our earlier work in [8]. Below we briefly describe the main concept and procedures.

Image demosaicing in Fig. 1 has been intensively researched in the past few decades to reconstruct the missing color samples due to the color filtering with good fidelity and less visible distortions. The state-of-the-art demosaicing algorithms often utilize the information of sensor samples from all three color channels and applied different reconstruction formulas on different edge types adaptively [3]. As each demosaicing algorithms likely introduces some unique and consistent image correlation among three color channels, detection of demosaicing regularity can be used for image forensics purposes.

In order to estimate the set of demosaicing formulas used, i.e. the derivative correlation weights, we first separate the reconstructed samples from sensor samples in $\mathbf{P}$. As Bayer CFAs in Fig. 1 are dominantly used commercially [3], we initially assume the first Bayer CFA is the underlying CFA and write

$$\mathbf{P} = \begin{pmatrix} \{r,G,B\}_{11} & \{R,g,B\}_{12} & \cdots \\ \{R,g,B\}_{21} & \{R,G,b\}_{22} & \\ \vdots & & \ddots \end{pmatrix}, \quad \mathbf{A} = \begin{pmatrix} a_{11} = r_{11} & a_{12} = g_{12} & \cdots \\ a_{21} = g_{21} & a_{22} = b_{22} & \\ \vdots & & \ddots \end{pmatrix} \quad (1)$$

where $\mathbf{A}$ denotes sensor samples and capital R, G, B represent the reconstructed samples. With a reverse classification technique [8], we classify all the reconstructed samples into 16 categories with known demosaicing directions so that each category contains the samples reconstructed by the similar formula. For the kth reconstructed sample X_{jk} of the jth category $\{D_{jk}\}$, we write a demosaicing equation below based on a partial second-order derivative correlation model.

$$e_{jk} = D''_{jk} - \mathbf{a}''^T_{jk}\mathbf{w}_j \quad (2)$$

Here, e_{jk} is the prediction error, D''_{jk} is the partial second-order derivative of D_{jk} computed on $\mathbf{P}$ along the demosaicing axis, $1 \leq j \leq 16$ and $1 \leq k \leq K$ with K denoting the size of the jth category. $\mathbf{a}''_{jk} \in \mathbb{R}^{c \times 1}$ denotes the support partial derivatives computed from the down-sampled $\mathbf{A}$. In the case that the jth category is on the red or blue color channels, $\mathbf{a}''_{jk}$ also include the support derivatives computed from the green channel. $\mathbf{w}_j \in \mathbb{R}^{c \times 1}$ is the vector of derivative weights, representing the applied demosaicing formula for the jth category and c is the number of weights chosen. The derivative correlation model is based on our observation that reconstructing a sample along one axis is equivalent to estimating its partial second-order derivative on a 2-by-2 periodical CFA lattice. For detection of the underlying demosaicing correlation, this model has the desired property of enabling estimating both intra-color channel and cross-channel demosaicing correlation with reduced detection variations caused by different image contents. Since for each sample in the jth category, we can write a similar equation to (2), by organizing all K equations into a matrix form, we have

$$\mathbf{e}_j = \mathbf{d}_j - \mathbf{Q}_j\mathbf{w}_j \quad (3)$$

where

$$\mathbf{e}_j = \begin{bmatrix} e_{j1} \\ \vdots \\ e_{jK} \end{bmatrix}, \quad \mathbf{d}_j = \begin{bmatrix} D''_{j1} \\ \vdots \\ D''_{jK} \end{bmatrix}, \quad \mathbf{Q}_j = \begin{bmatrix} \mathbf{a}''^T_{j1} \\ \vdots \\ \mathbf{a}''^T_{jK} \end{bmatrix}, \quad \mathbf{w}_j = \begin{bmatrix} w_{j1} \\ \vdots \\ w_{jm} \end{bmatrix}$$

Since $K \gg m$, the weights $\mathbf{w}_j$ is solved as a regularized least square solution below,

$$\min\left(\left\|\mathbf{e}_j\right\|^2 + \eta\left\|\mathbf{w}_j\right\|^2\right) \Rightarrow \mathbf{w}_j = \left(\mathbf{Q}_j{}^T\mathbf{Q}_j + \eta\mathbf{I}\right)^{-1}\mathbf{Q}_j\mathbf{d}_j \tag{4}$$

where η is a small regularization constant and $\mathbf{I} \in \mathbb{R}^{m \times m}$ denotes an identity matrix. By solving the weights separately for the 16 categories, we obtain a total of 312 weights. Also based on three other Bayer CFAs in Fig. 1, we repeat the weights estimation for three more times. Though the feature dimension increases 4 times to 1248, our features become more comprehensive [8] containing rich relative information. Not only representing the underlying set of demosaicing formulas used, our weights features also carry the distortion fingerprints caused by the post-demosaicing processing. We have demonstrated in [8] that our features can identify seven different types of post-demosaicing camera processes for a fixed Hamilton's demosaicing algorithm with a good accuracy. Therefore, our weights features characterize both the demosaicing process and the post-demosaicing processing.

2.3   Extraction of Eigen Weights

In view of the high feature dimensionality, which often incurs high computational cost, it is necessary to extract a limited number of desired features for our forensics analysis. In this section, we learn an eigen feature transformation for deriving a compact set of eigen weights. This is achieved by minimizing the within-image covariance and maximizing the between-image covariance, where the within-image eigen spectrum is regularized using [28] for increased reliability. Given M non-tampered training mobile images, each with $N=4$ cropped blocks, we let $\{\mathbf{x}_{mn}\}$, where $1 \leq m \leq M$ and $1 \leq n \leq N$, denote the normalized training feature vector. Here, a linear normalization is performed so that each feature has zero mean and unity variance. $\mathbf{x}_{mn} \in \mathbb{R}^{L \times 1}$ and $L=1248$ is our feature dimension. Our learning of eigen feature transformation is explained in the following steps:

1.   We compute the within-image covariance matrix $\mathbf{S}^{(\mathrm{w})}$ using

$$\mathbf{S}^{(\mathrm{w})} = \frac{1}{MN}\sum_{m=1}^{M}\sum_{n=1}^{N}\left(\mathbf{x}_{mn} - \bar{\mathbf{x}}_m\right)\left(\mathbf{x}_{mn} - \bar{\mathbf{x}}_m\right)^T \tag{5}$$

where $\bar{\mathbf{x}}_m = \frac{1}{N}\sum_{n=1}^{N}\mathbf{x}_{mn}$ is the mean vector of the mth image.

2.   We perform eigen decomposition using

$$\mathbf{\Lambda}^{(\mathrm{w})} = \mathbf{\Phi}^{(\mathrm{w})T}\mathbf{S}^{(\mathrm{w})}\mathbf{\Phi}^{(\mathrm{w})} \tag{6}$$

where $\mathbf{\Phi}^{(\mathrm{w})} = [\boldsymbol{\varphi}_1^{(\mathrm{w})},\ldots,\boldsymbol{\varphi}_L^{(\mathrm{w})}]$ is the eigenvector matrix of $\mathbf{S}^{(\mathrm{w})}$ and $\mathbf{\Lambda}^{(\mathrm{w})}$ is the diagonal matrix with the corresponding eigen values $\lambda_1^{(\mathrm{w})} \geq \lambda_2^{(\mathrm{w})} \geq \ldots \geq \lambda_L^{(\mathrm{w})}$ plotted as the training eigen spectrum in Fig. 4. Note in Fig. 4 that we can observe the widening gap in the log-scale plot between the training and the testing

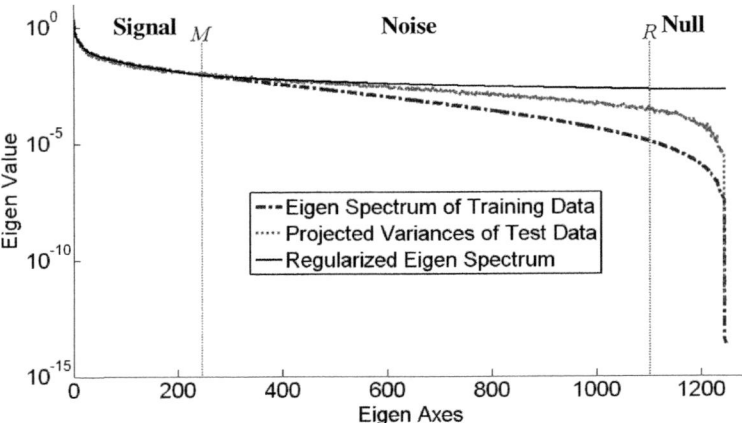

Fig. 4. Comparison of within-image eigen spectrum computed on a training mobile images, projected variances of the corresponding test mobile images and the regularized eigen spectrum

spectrums. This suggests that the eigen values learned in the training become less reliable and more susceptible to estimation errors. Since discriminant analysis often requires computing the inverse of these eigen values for feature scaling, the unreliable eigen spectrum need to be regularized;

3. Following the model in [28], we separate the eigen spectrum into 3 regions, "signal", "noise" and "null", and fit a regularized spectrum as plotted in Fig. 4. By choosing several model parameters M, R, α and β according to [28], the regularized eigen value corresponding to the ℓth eigenvector is written as [28].

$$\tilde{\lambda}_\ell^{(w)} = \begin{cases} \lambda_\ell^{(w)}, & \ell < M \\ \alpha/(\ell+\beta), & M \leq \ell \leq R \\ \alpha/(1+R+\beta), & R < \ell \leq L \end{cases} \tag{7}$$

4. We perform the whitening feature transformation using

$$\mathbf{y}_{mn} = \tilde{\mathbf{\Psi}}_L^{(w)T} \mathbf{x}_{mn} \tag{8}$$

where $\tilde{\mathbf{\Psi}}_L^{(w)} = \left[\boldsymbol{\varphi}_1^{(w)} / \sqrt{\tilde{\lambda}_1^{(w)}}, \ldots, \boldsymbol{\varphi}_L^{(w)} / \sqrt{\tilde{\lambda}_L^{(w)}} \right]$.

5. Based on the $\{\mathbf{y}_{mn}\}$, we compute the total covariance matrix using

$$\mathbf{S}^{(t)} = \frac{1}{MN} \sum_{m=1}^{M} \sum_{n=1}^{N} \left(\mathbf{y}_{mn} - \bar{\mathbf{y}} \right) \left(\mathbf{y}_{mn} - \bar{\mathbf{y}} \right)^T \tag{9}$$

where $\bar{\mathbf{y}} = \frac{1}{MN} \sum_{m=1}^{M} \sum_{n=1}^{N} \mathbf{y}_{mn}$ is the global mean vector.

6. We then perform eigen decomposition on $\mathbf{S}^{(t)}$ and construct $\tilde{\mathbf{\Psi}}_E^{(t)} = [\boldsymbol{\varphi}_1^{(t)},\dots,\boldsymbol{\varphi}_E^{(t)}]$ for feature reduction using principal component analysis (PCA), where typically $E \ll L$. $\boldsymbol{\varphi}_1^{(t)},\dots,\boldsymbol{\varphi}_E^{(t)}$ are the leading eigenvectors of $\mathbf{S}^{(t)}$ corresponding to the E largest eigenvalues. The compact eigen weights vector

$$\mathbf{z}_{mn} = \tilde{\mathbf{\Psi}}_E^{(t)T} \mathbf{y}_{mn} = \mathbf{F}\mathbf{x}_{mn} \tag{10}$$

where $\mathbf{z}_{mn} \in \mathbb{R}^{E\times 1}$ and our learned eigen transformation $\mathbf{F} = \left(\tilde{\mathbf{\Psi}}_L^{(w)} \tilde{\mathbf{\Psi}}_E^{(t)} \right)^T$.

2.4   Measurement of the Inconsistency

Let $\mathbf{z}_1,\dots,\mathbf{z}_n,\dots,\mathbf{z}_N$, where $\mathbf{z}_n \in \mathbb{R}^{E\times 1}$, be the eigen weights vectors corresponding to all the sampled blocks from a given test mobile image. We compute the covariance matrix

$$\mathbf{Z} = \frac{1}{N}\sum\nolimits_{n=1}^{N}\left(\mathbf{z}_n - \overline{\mathbf{z}}\right)\left(\mathbf{z}_n - \overline{\mathbf{z}}\right)^T \tag{11}$$

where $\overline{z} = \frac{1}{N}\sum\nolimits_{n=1}^{N}\mathbf{z}_n$ is the mean vector. We propose to measure the correlation inconsistency by

$$J = \sqrt{\text{Trace}\left(\mathbf{Z}\right)} \tag{12}$$

This metric quantifies the total variance of the eigen feature vectors extracted from the sampled blocks.

Since our derivative weights features model both the underlying demosaicing formulas used and its post-processing, our features estimated from different regions of an intact image are supposedly identical in an ideal case. However, the different image contents would inevitably affect our estimated weights and contribute to an increased within-image covariance. Through regularizing the within-image eigen spectrum, performing whitening transformation and PCA feature reduction, our derived eigen weights features are expectedly insensitive to within-image content variations and highly sensitive to the image signal mixing from multiple image sources. Our proposed metric J, hence, translates to a small value for a non-tampered mobile image and a large value for a tampered image, where some sampled blocks are transplanted from other image sources. The decision threshold for using J to detect the presence of tampering can be determined from some training statistics of a representative mobile image dataset.

3   Experimental Results

Our mobile image set constructed for the experiments contains 1000 images from a total of 10 mobile cameras from 6 brands in Table 1, where cameras of identical or

Table 1. Mobile cameras used

ID	Brand	Model	Image Dimension
N1		5300	1280×960
N2		5300	1280×960
N3	Nokia	N73	2048×1536
N4		N73	2048×1536
N5		N73	2048×1536
SE6	Sony Ericsson	K750c	1632×1224
M7	Motorola	L6	640×480
D8	Dopod	P3600i	1600×1200
O9	O2	XDA	1200×1600
S10	Sumsung	SGH i780	1600×1200

Fig. 5. Sample mobile images

close models are present. Each camera has 100 mobile images. We collect these images from a number of contributors, which are taken by their personal cellular phones and all images are the direct camera outputs stored in the default JPEG format. These images cover a large variety of common indoor and outdoor scenes captured under different lighting conditions. Fig. 5 shows several representative image samples from different mobile cameras. We randomly select 500 images, with 50 from each camera, to learn the eigenfeature transformation and the remaining images are reserved for testing. As tabulated in Table 2, we also generate another set of tampered images by modifying the intact test images from four source cameras of different models. Each tampered image is created from an intact test Image A by replacing one of its four sampled blocks randomly with a block from a different Image B. For each of the four Image-A sources, we create 7 or 8 times of tampered test images by considering different Image-B source cameras.

Note that we have included some Image-B sources of the identical camera and of the same model as their correpsonding Image-A sources when the tampered dataset is constructed. The rational is that two images acquired from the same camera are also likely to contain some processing differences due to the different adaptive parameters used. For instance, the white balancing parameters used are often adaptive to the measured color temperature on the scene content. Other processing parameters can also be adaptive due to different camera settings, such as the scene mode, ISO, flash, etc. Besides these, different cameras of the same model also likely contain some statistical differences. Our previous work in [9] shows that three Nokia N73 can be identified with more than 80% accuracy rate using similar demosaicing features. Though this rate is significantly lower than that for different camera models, it suggests that some weak differences exist among cameras of the same model. Similarly, the result in [15] also shows that two Sony K700 cameras can be identified

Table 2. Dataset of the tampered images, where one of the four sampled blocks from Image A is replaced with a randomly sampled block from a different Image B. Refer to Table 1 for the source cameras.

Source camera (Image A)	Source camera (Image B)							
N1	N1	N2	N3	SE6	M7	D8	O9	S10
N3	N3	N4	N1	SE6	M7	D8	O9	S10
SE6	SE6	N1	N3	M7	D8	O9	S10	-
M7	M7	N1	N3	SE6	D8	O9	S10	-

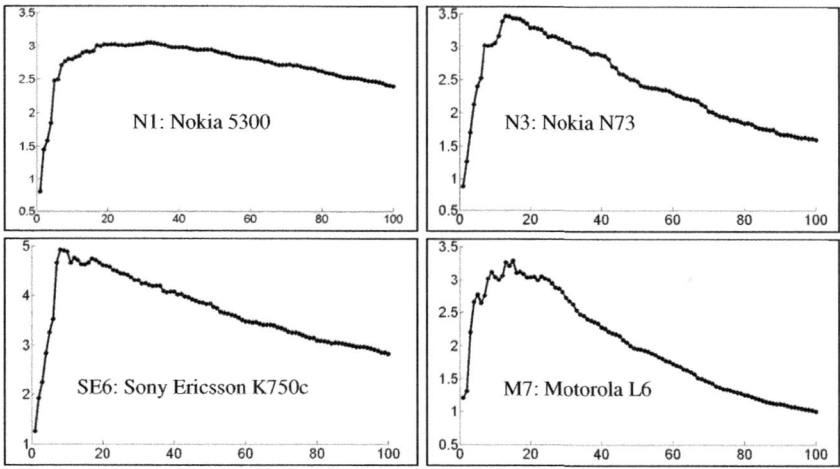

Fig. 6. Fisher's ratio [29] versus number of eigen weights for different sources

with over 90% accuracy using other statistical features. These differences can translate to feature-domain differences in our estimated derivative weights and contribute to positive tamper detection performance. By including the similar tampering sources, it allows us testing the difficult tamper detection scenarios when images sharing very similar processing regularity are combined.

3.1   Determining the Number of Eigen Features

Based on our learned eigen feature transformation (EFT), we vary the number of eigen features E and compute the statistics of our measured inconsistencies separately for the different sources in Table 2. For a given E, we let $\mu_g(E)$ and $v_g(E)$ denote the mean and variance, respectively, of the inconsistencies for the intact images. $\mu_t(E)$ and $v_t(E)$ are for the tampered images. We then compute the Fisher's ratio [29] using

$$f(E) = \frac{\left(\mu_g(E) - \mu_t(E)\right)^2}{v_g(E) + v_t(E)} \tag{13}$$

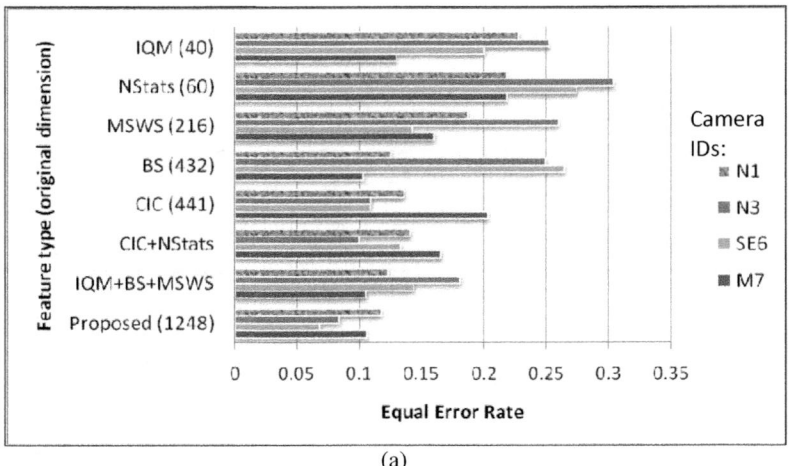

(a)

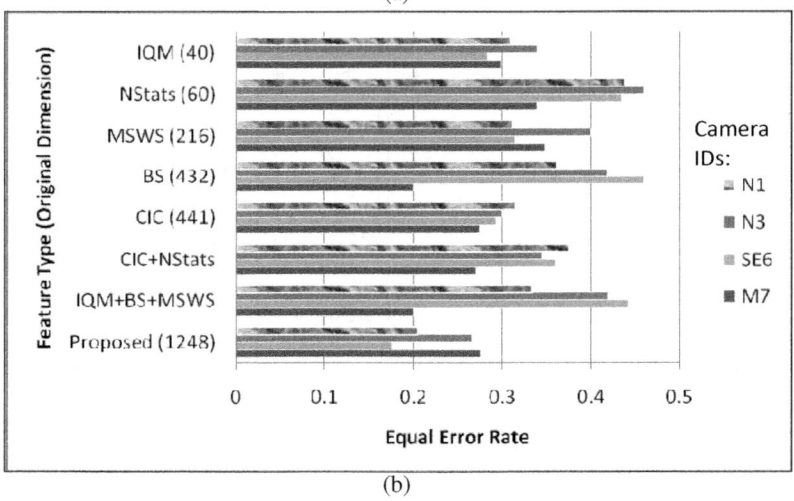

(b)

Fig. 7. Performance comparisons in term of equal error rate (%) for tamper detection on different source mobile cameras, based on (a) selected eigen features and (b) the original features, respectively

to measure the discriminant power of our proposed metric. Fig. 6 plots Fisher's ratio versus number of eigen weights E for the 4 different sources. From Fig. 6, we can see that the Fisher's ratio increases quickly initially to the maximal value and starts decreasing gradually when E is increased from 1 to 100. Based on these results, we choose $E=14$ for our eigen weights features in the following experiments.

3.2   Tamper Detection

We first compare our eigen weights features with the eigen features extracted from several other sets of forensics features in terms of equal error rates (EER) for tamper detection. These other feature sets include multi-scale wavelet statistics (MSWS)

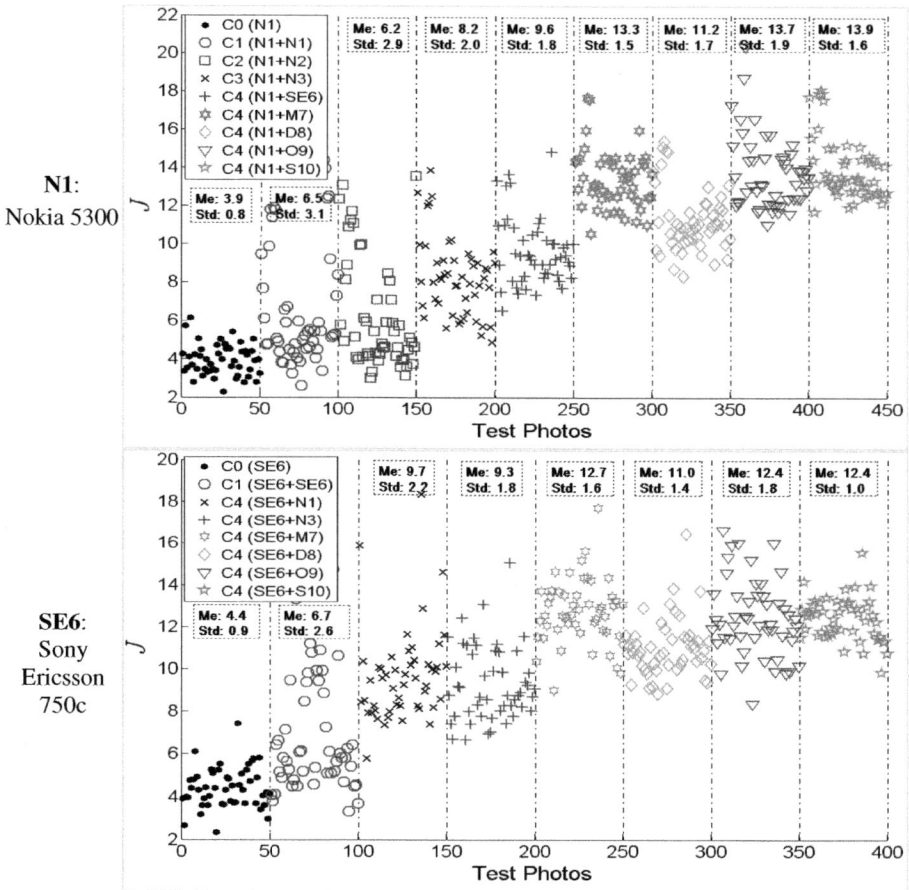

Fig. 8. Scatter plots of measured inconsistencies for the intact and the tampered images from two different camera sources

[15, 17], binary similarities (BS) [14, 15, 17, 30], image quality metrics (IQM) [13, 15-17], color interpolation coefficients (CIC) [4, 5], noise statistics (NStats) [5], the combination of MSWS, BS and IQM [15] and the combination of CIC and NStats [5]. Based on the description in [15], we compute a total of 432 BS features. Though this number is still less than the 480 BS features used in [15], our BS feature set covers majority of the BS features. We conducted the similar experiments as in Fig. 6 to determine the number of eigen features required for other feature types. We use 3, 5 and 6 eigen features, respectively, for NStats, IQM and MSWS. For the remaining feature types, we use 12-14 eigen features. The best number of eigen features is likely related with several factors including the number of camera sources, the number of sampled blocks and the discriminative power of the feature types. Based on the eigen feature size, the EERs are compared in Fig. 7(a) for tamper detection using different Image-A sources. For source camera N1, N3 and SE6, our eigen weights features consistently give the best EERs. For M7, whose images are of relatively low quality,

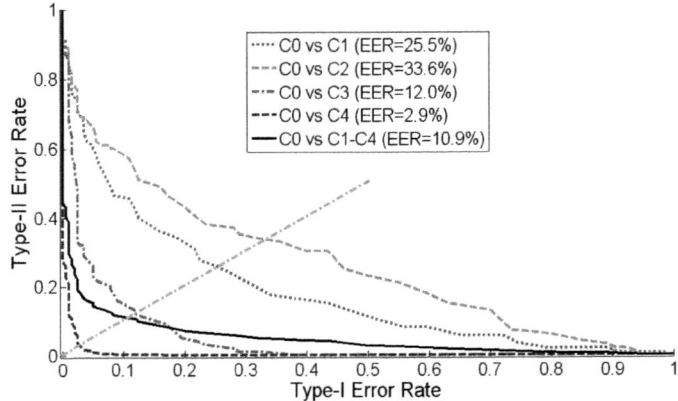

Fig. 9. Receiver operation characteristic (ROC) curves for discriminating intact photos and different classes of tampered photos. Type-I error rate is the percentage of non-tampered photos being misclassified as tampered. Type-II error rate is the percentage of tampered photos being misclassified as non-tampered.

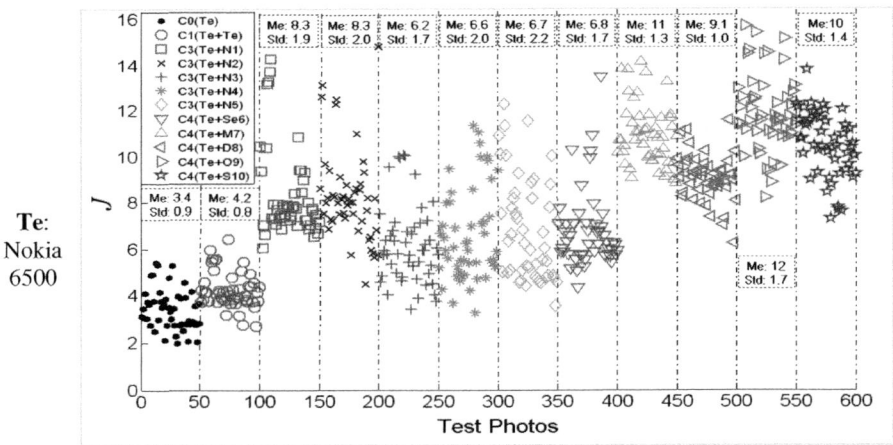

Fig. 10. Scatter plots of measured inconsistencies for the intact and the tampered images from an unseen Nokia 6500 camera model

our proposed eigen features perform slightly inferior to the eigen BS features. In Fig. 7(b), we also show the tamper detection performance when the learnt EFT is not applied. Comparing Fig. 7(a) and (b), we can see that EFT not only consistently reduces the EER for our proposed weights features, but also works well for all other types of statistical features. On average, EFT achieves 51.1%'s reduction of the EERs with significantly less number of features required for inconsistency measurement.

We also differentiate five classes of images including C0 (non-tampered images), C1 (tampered with Image-A and B from the same camera), C2 (different cameras of the same model), C3 (different models of the same brand) and C4 (different brands). From the scatter plots in Fig. 8, we observe much higher mean and standard deviations for Class C1 and C2's statistics than that for the intact C0 class. The tampered classes C3 or C4 are visually easy to be separated from the intact Class C0. Practically, it is desirable to detect image tampering blindly such that the source camera information is not required. We put the non-tampered and the tampered statistics from 4 different Image-A sources together to study the source-independent tampering detection performance. Fig. 9 shows our receiver operating characteristics (ROC) curves for identifying different tampering classes. As expected, C1 and C2 tampering are harder to detect due to very similar camera processing pipelines. Our detection is reliable for Class C3 and C4. Especially we achieve a low EER of 2.9% for C4. Based on a common decision threshold, the overall EER of 10.9% also suggests a satisfactory performance for detecting the group of C1 to C4 image tampering.

We have also simulated the tamper detection scenario on images from an unseen Nokia 6500 camera model, whose images are not included in learning the EFT. The tamper detection results in Fig. 10 show a similar trend as the scatter plots shown in Fig. 8 that most C3 and C4 tampered image groups are visually easy to be separated from the intact Class C0. Among the three C3 groups with the lowest mean inconsistencies, their Image-B sources are cameras from a same Nokia N73 model. This suggests that Nokia 6500 model likely shares a greater deal of processing similarity with Nokia N73 model. A satisfactory EER of 12.0% is achieved, which is only 1.7% higher than 10.3%, the EER that we can achieve if we include the images from this Nokia 6500 model in learning the eigenfeature transformation (EFT). The small EER increment shows that the eigenfeature transformation learned based on other camera models is largely applicable to the unseen Nokia 6500 camera. Therefore, we do not need to exhaust all available mobile camera models in learning the eigenfeature transformation as long as our training image set is representative and comprehensive enough covering a good variety of different mobile camera sources and different scenery.

Though our proposed method achieves confident performance in detecting C3 and C4 types of tampering, the detection results in Fig. 8, 9 and 10 are expectedly less satisfactory for the C1 and C2 tampering types, where the Image-A and B share very similar pipelines. In such cases, we still note that the EERs of 25.5% and 33.6% in Fig. 9 are still much lower than 50%, the worst scenario corresponding to random guess. This confirms that even two images from the same camera can contain some extent of correlation differences due to the different adaptive processing parameters. However, this difference is not significant enough to ensure reliable detection of C1 and C2 tampering types. To make the tamper detection more comprehensive, the forensics analysts can use our proposed method as a pre-filtering step to remove majority of tampered images and to limit the range of the potential Image-B sources for the reminder of images. Then, they can apply some other techniques, e.g. sensor noise pattern approaches [10, 11, 12] and splicing boundary detection approaches [18, 23], to check out for other tampering clues by providing additional resources and human assistance.

3.3   Sensitivity Analysis

Sampling block size and the percentage of our sampled blocks falling into the tampered area are two important parameters that govern the detection sensitivity on

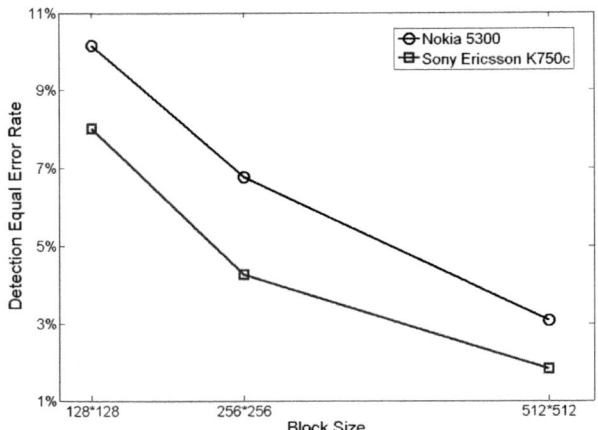

Fig. 11. Detection Equal Error Rate versus Sampling Block Size

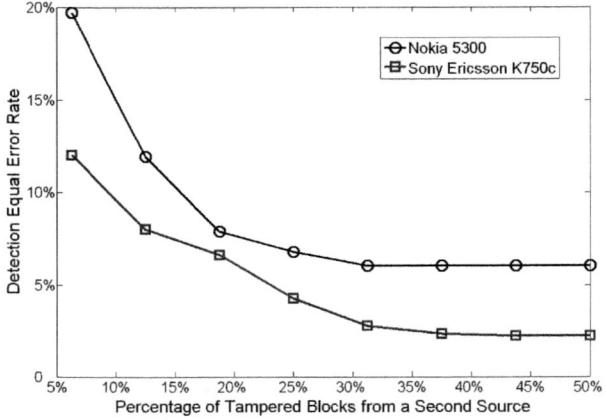

Fig. 12. Detection Equal Error Rate versus Percentage of Tampered Blocks from a Second Source Model

relatively small-area tampering. Also in a more practical scenario, a sampled block may be partially tampered with only a certain percentage of area being replaced by an image from another source. In this section, we vary these parameters to analyze how our detection performances for N1 and SE6 cameras are affected. For both cameras, we reconstruct their tampered image sets by including only the Image-B sources of different camera models or brands in Figure 10. As a result, the corresponding tampered images are 8 and 9 times of the untampered images for the N1 and SE6 cameras, respectively.

In the first experiment, by fixing the total coverage area of the sampled blocks and the percentage of tampered blocks from a second source model as 25%, we reduce the block size from 512×512 to 256×256 and 128×128. Here, a small block size of 128×128 would correspond to a total of 64 non-overlapping sampled blocks while a block size of 512×512 corresponds to 4 blocks. Fig. 11 plots the tamper detection

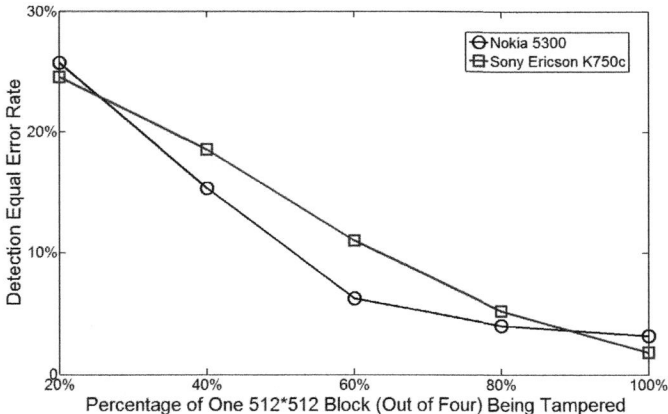

Fig. 13. Detection Equal Error Rate versus Percentage of Tampered Area in One of Four Cropped Blocks of Size 512×512

EER versus the block sizes. From the figure, we can see that lowest EERs are achieved with the largest block size for both cameras. The EERs increase consistently when we reduce the block size. Since a larger block generally provides more color samples and content variations, our derivative weights can be better estimated statistically with less content-dependant variations in a large block than in a relatively small block. Therefore, larger block sizes lead to better tamper detection performance. Our study also shows that even with a small block size of 128×128, we can still achieve reasonable tamper detection EERs of 10.2% and 8% for the N1 and SE6 cameras, respectively.

In the second experiment, by fixing the total number of sampled blocks as 16 and the block size as 256×256, we study the detection performance when the number of tampered blocks, which are transplanted from a second camera source, is gradually increased from 1 to 8. As shown in Fig. 12, the detection EERs drop sharply initially and become relatively stabilized when the percentage of tampered blocks exceeds 30%. Even with a small 12.5% of tampered blocks, our tamper detection EERs can still be as low as 11.9% and 6.8% for the N1 and SE6 cameras, respectively.

In the third experiment, we study the tamper detection when only one out of four sampled 512×512 blocks is tampered partially. In this block, the alien image portion transplanted from a different source would also affect our estimated weights at the feature extraction level and lead to an increment in our measured inconsistency. The amount of increment is closely related with size of the tampered area. As shown in Figure 13, the larger the percentage of the tampered area in a block, the lower is our achieved EER rates. When 60% area of one sampled block is tampered, our detection error rates will still remain as low as 6.3% and 11.0% for the N1 and SE6 cameras, respectively.

4   Conclusions

In this paper, we propose a novel framework to quantify the statistical correlation inconsistency on a mobile image by measuring the variations of our eigen weights features from a set of sampled blocks at different image locations. Through regularizing and minimizing the within-image covariance, comparison results show that our eigen weights perform better than several other sets of forensics features in detecting the presence of tampering. Our methods show a good reliability in detecting the C3 and C4 types of tampered images in a blind context, where information of the source mobile camera is not required. Especially, we achieve a low EER of 2.9% for detecting C4 tampering class. These suggest that our proposed method has a good confidence to detect the presence of tampering when one of the four sampled block is from a different mobile camera model or brand. However, for C1 and C2 types of tampering, which involves image signal mixing from very similar processing pipelines, our current result still requires further improvement to be practical. The sensitivity analysis shows that though large sampling block size, e.g. 512×512, typically gives better tamper detection performance, a small block size of 128×128 can still lead to reasonably good detection EERs of 8-10%.

Our work can be extended further along several avenues. First, our tamper detection method can be applied to digital images acquired by other devices, such as DSCs. Second, it is interesting to investigate other forms of tampering inconsistencies besides mixing image signals. Third, more adaptive block sampling schemes with smaller block sizes shall be investigated. Fourth, localization of the blocks affected by tampering can be a good additional feature to be included.

References

1. Mosleh, F. (kodak): Cameras in Handsets Evolving from Novelty to DSC Performance, Despite Constraints. Embedded.com (2008)
2. Lewis, J.: Don't Just Stand and Stare, Shoot it, Too. The Singapore Straits Times, April 28 (2007)
3. Li, X., Gunturk, B., Zhang, L.: Image Demosaicing: a Systematic Survey. In: Proc. of SPIE, vol. 6822 (2008)
4. Swaminathan, A., Wu, M., Liu, K.J.R.: Nonintrusive Component Forensics of Visual Sensors Using Output Images. IEEE Trans. on Information Forensics and Security 2(1), 91–106 (2007)
5. McKay, C., Swaminathan, A., Gou, H., Wu, M.: Image Acquisition Forensics: Forensic Analysis to Identify Imaging Source. In: Proc. of ICASSP, pp. 1657–1660 (2008)
6. Swaminathan, A., Wu, M., Liu, K.J.R.: Digital Image Forensics via Intrinsic Fingerprints. IEEE Trans. on Information Forensics and Security 3(1), 101–117 (2008)
7. Cao, H., Kot, A.C.: A Generalized Model for Detection of Demosaicing Characteristics. In: Proc. of ICME, pp. 1513–1516 (2008)
8. Cao, H., Kot, A.C.: Accurate Detection of Demosaicing Regularity for Digital Image Forensics. IEEE Trans. on Information Forensics and Security 4(4), 899–910 (2009)
9. Cao, H., Kot, A.C.: Mobile Camera Identification Using Demosaicing Features. In: Proc. of ISCAS, pp. 1683–1686 (2010)

10. Lucas, J., Fridrich, J., Goljan, M.: Digital Camera Identification from Sensor Pattern Noise. IEEE Trans. Information Forensics and Security 1(2), 205–214 (2006)
11. Chen, M., Fridrich, J., Goljan, M., Lucas, J.: Determining Image Origin and Integrity Using Sensor Noise. IEEE Trans. on Information Forensics and Security 3(1), 74–89 (2008)
12. Alles, E.J., Geradts, Z.J.M.H., Veenman, C.J.: Source Camera Identification for Low Resolution Heavily Compressed Images. In: Proc. of ICCSA, pp. 557–567 (2008)
13. Tsai, M.-J., Lai, C.-L., Liu, J.: Camera/Mobile Phone Source Identification for Digital Forensics. In: Proc. of ICASSP, vol. 2, pp. 221–224 (2007)
14. Avcibas, I., Kharrazi, M., Memon, N., Sankur, B.: Image Steganalysis with Binary Similarity Measures. EUROSIP Journal of Applied Signal Processing 17, 2749–2757 (2005)
15. Celiktutan, O., Sankur, B., Avcibas, I.: Blind Identification of Source Cell-Phone Model. IEEE Trans. on Information Forensics and Security 3(3), 553–566 (2008)
16. Avcibas, I., Bayram, S., Memon, N., Ramkumar, M., Sankur, B.: A Classifier Design for Detecting Image Manipulations. In: Proc. of ICIP, vol. 4, pp. 2645–2648 (2004)
17. Bayram, S., Avcibas, I., Sankur, B., Memon, N.: Image Manipulation Detection. Journal of Electronic Imaging 15, 41102 (2006)
18. Ng, T.-T., Chang, S.-F., Sun, Q.: Blind Detection of Photomontage Using High Order Statistics. In: Proc. of ISCAS, vol. 5, pp. 688–691 (2004)
19. Johnson, M.K., Farid, H.: Exposing Digital Forgeries by Detecting Inconsistencies in Lighting. In: Proc. of ACM Multimedia Security Workshop, pp. 1–10 (2005)
20. Farid, H.: A Survey of Image Forgery Detection. IEEE Signal Processing Magazine 26(2), 16–25 (2009)
21. He, J., Lin, Z., Wang, L., Tang, X.: Detecting Doctored JPEG Images via DCT Coefficient Analysis. In: Leonardis, A., Bischof, H., Pinz, A. (eds.) ECCV 2006, Part III. LNCS, vol. 3953, pp. 423–435. Springer, Heidelberg (2006)
22. Fu, D., Shi, Y.Q., Su, W.: A Generalized Benford's Law for JPEG Coefficients and its Applications in Image Forensics. In: Proc. of SPIE, vol. 6505, p. 65051L (2007)
23. Chen, W., Shi, Y.Q.: Image Splicing Detection Using 2-D Phase Congruency and Statistical Moments of Characteristic Function. In: Proc. of SPIE, vol. 6505, p. 65050R (2007)
24. Luo, W., Qu, Z., Huang, J., Qiu, G.: A Novel Method for Detecting Cropped and Recompressed Image Blocks. In: Proc. of ICASSP 2007, vol. 2, pp. 217–220 (2007)
25. Barni, M., Costanzo, L., Sabatini, L.: Identification of Cut & Paste Tampering by Means of Double-JPEG Detection and Image Segmentation. In: Proc. of ISCAS 2010, pp. 1687–1690 (2010)
26. Li, C.-T.: Source Camera Identification Using Enhanced Sensor Pattern Noise. IEEE Trans. on Information Forensics and Security 5(2), 280–287 (2010)
27. Mahdian, B., Saic, S.: A Bibliography on Blind Methods for Identifying Image Forgery. Signal Processing: Image Communication 25(6), 389–399 (2010)
28. Jiang, X., Mandal, B., Kot, A.C.: Eigenfeature Regularization and Extraction in Face Recognition. IEEE Trans. on Pattern Analysis and Machine Intelligence 30(3), 383–394 (2008)
29. Duda, O., Hart, P.E., Stork, D.G.: Pattern Classification, 2nd edn. John Wiley & Sons, New York (2001)
30. Kharrazi, M., Sencar, H.T., Memon, N.: Improving Steganalysis by Fusion Techniques: A Case Study with Image Steganography. In: Shi, Y.Q. (ed.) Transactions on DHMS I. LNCS, vol. 4300, pp. 123–137. Springer, Heidelberg (2006)

Secure Steganography Using Randomized Cropping

Arijit Sur[1,*], Vignesh Ramanathan[2], and Jayanta Mukherjee[3]

[1] Department of Computer Science and Engineering,
Indian Institute of Technology, Guwahati-781039, India
arijit@iitg.ernet.in
[2] Department of Electrical Engineering,
Indian Institute of Technology, Kharagpur-721302, India
vigneshram.iitkgp@gmail.com
[3] Department of Computer Science and Engineering,
Indian Institute of Technology, Kharagpur-721302, India
jay@cse.iitkgp.ernet.in

Abstract. In this paper[1], a novel steganographic scheme is proposed, where embedding is done adaptively in image regions with high level of high frequency component. The steganalytic detection performance becomes poorer as these high frequency components mask the steganographic embedding noise. The security of the proposed scheme is further increased by separating the embedding domain from the steganalytic domain. This separation is done by randomizing the embedding domain using a new concept called randomized cropping. State of the art spatial domain steganalyzers are considered to evaluate the security of the proposed scheme. The LSB matching algorithm is used for steganographic embedding. It is shown experimentally that the LSB matching algorithm wrapped with proposed scheme performs comparatively better than simple LSB matching scheme, against the steganalytic attacks under consideration.

Keywords: Steganography, blind attack, spatial domain steganography, high frequency noise, LSB matching algorithm.

1 Introduction

Steganography is the art of hiding information in innocent looking cover objects and thus visual and statistical undetectability is one of the major concerns in steganographic research. On the other hand, steganalysis is the science of detecting stego content in innocent looking objects. A comprehensive survey on steganography and sateganalysis can be found in [1]. In this paper, we have concentrated on $\pm k$ steganography. In steganographic literature, $\pm k$ steganography generally implies that the embedding distortion for a pixel or coefficient

---

* Corresponding author.

[1] The first author gratefully acknowledge the support received from Infosys Technologies Ltd., Bangalore, under the Infosys Fellowship Award.

Y.Q. Shi (Ed.): Transactions on DHMS VII, LNCS 7110, pp. 82–95, 2012.

is at most $+k$ or $-k$. One simple example of $\pm k$ steganography is LSB matching where k=1. The steganalysis attacks on $\pm k$ steganography are broadly classified into two major groups. Firstly, the targeted attacks, where the steganographic algorithm is known to the attacker and secondly, the blind attacks where, steganalysis is independent of steganographic algorithms. Here, we have considered two blind attacks [2 & 3] and two targeted attacks [4 & 5] on $\pm k$ steganography. In Wavelet Absolute Moment (WAM) steganalyzer [2], Fridrich et al. have used higher order moments of wavelet domain noise residual as the steganalytic features. Moulin, in [3], advocated the use of empirical PDF (probability density function) and CF (Characteristic Function) moments as features to train the steganalytic classifier. In case of targeted attacks on LSB matching, Jun Zhang et al 's high frequency noise based attack [4] and Fangjun Huang et al 's targeted attack [5] can efficiently detect the presence of steganographic embedding specially when never compressed images are used as cover.

Spatial domain blind steganalysis generally extracts steganalytic features from the noise residuals. In the presence of high level of high frequency component, the performance of classifiers become poorer as the high frequency components effectively mask the steganographic noise [4]. So it may be a good idea to adaptively embed the data bits in image regions with more high frequency content. In this paper, we propose a new steganographic scheme which attempts to resist the spatial domain steganalytic attacks by embedding bits in image regions containing adequate high frequency components. High frequency sub bands obtained in wavelet sub band decomposition are used for embedding as a global adaptive criterion. The choice of high frequency image regions is further tuned using a local adaptive criterion where wavelet coefficients from selected sub bands are used for embedding if they are greater than a prescribed threshold. Again, it is well known that the performance of blind steganalysis is reduced if embedding domain can be separated from steganalytic domain [6]. In this YASS scheme [6], authors have shown that calibration of macroscopic properties becomes useless if embedding domain is separated from channel domain. Here embedding domain means the domain where actual embedding is done. On the other hand, steganalytic domain implies the domain which is assumed as embedding domain by attackers or steganalyzers. So in other words, the process of steganalytic attacks become complicated if attacker doest not know the exact embedding domain. Targeted attacks also become complicated if proper embedding domain is unknown to the attacker. In the proposed scheme, the separation of the embedding domain from steganalytic domain is achieved by a novel concept called randomized copping. A new steganographic algorithm called *Steganographic Algorithm with Randomized Cropping (SARC)* based on the same idea has been proposed in this paper. It is found that LSB matching wrapped with proposed scheme greatly outperforms the simple LSB matching algorithm against the targeted as well as blind attacks. The proposed scheme is not compared with the YASS [6] scheme, as the the YASS algorithm is a JPEG domain scheme while the proposed *SARC* scheme is a spatial domain scheme. In the YASS scheme [6], embedding domain is separated from the channel domain by randomly selecting 8×8 blocks at different locations and embedding the data in the DCT coefficients using the QIM [10] while in the proposed scheme, embedding domain is obtained by random cropping of pixels from spatial domain and subsequent integer wavelet transformation of the cropped image. After embedding, the embedded image is brought back to the spatial domain for communication. Thus embedded image is communicated as a spatial domain image. Since embedded images are spatial domain images, the steganalytic attacks suitable for YASS (mostly JPEG based blind attacks) are not very suitable for the proposed scheme. The rest of the paper is organized as follows: in Section 2, a detailed discussion on randomized cropping will be presented. The proposed embedding and extraction scheme is presented in section 3. The experimental resuls are presented in section 4. The paper is concluded in section 5.

2   Randomized Cropping

Randomized cropping is a process for separating out the embedding domain from steganalytic domain by randomizing the spatial distribution of the image pixels.

2.1   Procedure of Randomized Cropping

In randomized cropping, image pixels are pseudo randomly removed or cropped from the image matrix in order to remove (or crop) an entire row or column. For an example, cropping one pixel from each column would lead to removal of an entire row from the image matrix. A column can be removed similarly by cropping one pixel from each row. An example of row cropping (random removal of one pixel from each column) and subsequent column cropping (random removal of one pixel from each row) has been described in the Figure 1. The pixels can be replaced after data is embedded in the cropped image, hence any visual defects due to cropping can be repaired.

2.2   Analysis of Randomized Cropping

Randomized cropping is implemented in the proposed scheme, such that n rows and m columns are cropped where m and n are any two positive integers. Let I be an $M \times N$ image matrix with M rows and N columns. If one row is cropped from the matrix, the resultant image matrix size would be $(M - 1) \times N$. Since one pixel is cropped from different locations of the each columns, without loss of generality, this operation is equivalent to cropping a single row and produces a $(M - 1) \times N$ matrix. The locations from which pixels are cropped for each column are determined by a pseudorandom number generator ($PRNG$) which can produce PRN sequence in the range $1 \ldots N$. Similarly, a column can be cropped from $(M - 1) \times N$ matrix using another PRN sequence ranging from $1 \ldots M - 1$, producing another matrix of size $(M - 1) \times (N - 1)$. The seeds of these pseudorandom sequences will be shared secrets to the sender and the receiver. The seed of the $PRNG$ is known to the receiver end; hence the pixels

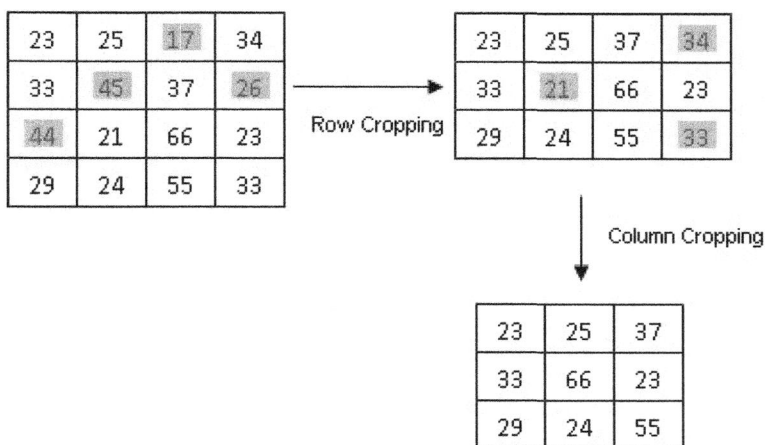

Fig. 1. Block Diagram of Randomized Cropping

can be cropped before extraction of data from the image. For an $M \times N$ image, the spatial distribution of the image pixels can be rearranged in $M^N \times N^{M-1}$ different ways with the above procedure of cropping one single row first and then one single column. If two rows and two columns have been randomly cropped (say the cropping dimension is $m = 2$ and $n = 2$), the space is $M^N \times N^{M-1} \times M - 1^{N-1} \times N - 1^{M-2}$. In our experiments, randomized cropping is used with the cropping dimension $m = 2$ and $n = 2$. The proposed scheme uses the Integer Wavelet (IW) domain for embedding data. The IW domain which is seen by the steganalyzers is different from the IW domain where actual embedding is done because of randomization of embedding domain by the proposed randomized cropping operation.

2.3   Impact of Randomized Cropping Operation on IWT Domain

How does the proposed randomized cropping operation actually randomize the integer wavelet coefficients is an important issue. Intuitively, the proposed operation change the integer wavelet coefficients. This fact can be verified experimentally by analyzing the differences among four sub bands obtained through IWT decomposition of the portion of the original image and randomly cropped image I_r. To keep the part of the original image of same size, we considered the topmost and leftmost part of it of size $[(M-2) \times (N-2)]$. The mean and variance of the difference in coefficient values between the four sub bands (HH, HL, LH and LL) of I and I_r are given in Table 1. The values are averaged over 1000 different randomized cropping permutations for the uncompressed image database. The histogram of the difference between the four bands of the original image I and the randomly cropped image I_r is also shown in Figure 2.

From above table and figures, it is observed that there are substantial difference in the different IWT sub-bands due the randomized cropping operation.

Table 1. Mean and Variance of coefficient value difference between the four sub bands of the original and cropped image

Sub Band	Mean	Variance
HH	8.6113	246.8256
HL	9.1605	447.1398
LH	14.1030	796.6184
LL	5.4152	112.6543

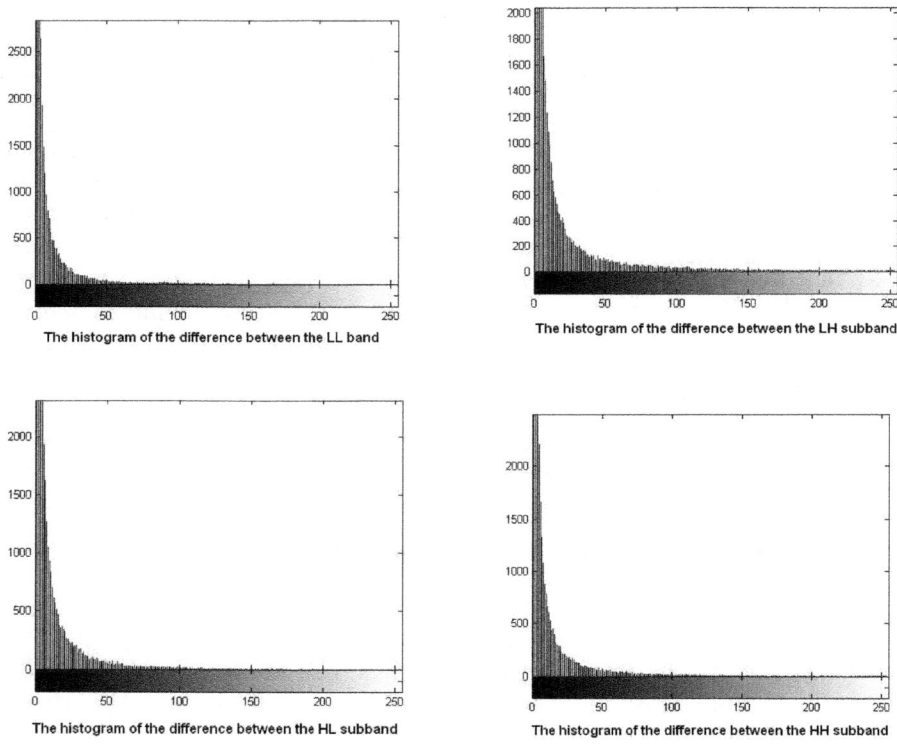

Fig. 2. The Histogram of the Difference between the Four Sub-bands

For example, if cropping dimension $m = 2$ and $n = 2$ (e.g. cropping 2 rows and 2 columns), $M^N \times N^{M-1} \times M - 1^{N-1} \times N - 1^{M-2}$ numbers of different IWT coefficient domains can be obtained. Each domain has substantial differences with other domains. If the attacker does not have the secret seeds for randomized cropping operation, they can't find the exact embedding domain. This makes the scheme more secure by increasing complication in the steganalytic process.

3   Proposed Scheme

3.1   Embedding Scheme

In the proposed algorithm, high frequency regions in the cover image are determined globally using high frequency sub-bands in wavelet sub-band decomposition. Integer wavelet domain is used for the embedding. IWT coefficients are obtained using the *Lifting Scheme* [9] which ensures perfect reconstruction. The integer wavelet coefficients [8], specifically from HH, HL and LH bands, are used for the embedding. All coefficients from these sub bands are not used for the embedding. A predefined threshold value is considered. Coefficients those are greater than that of threshold value, are used for embedding. This local adaptive criterion further improves the selection of high frequency image regions for data embedding. During embedding, the value of a selected coefficient which was initially (before embedding) above the threshold, may become below the threshold due to embedding. In such a situation, a suitable value is added to that stego coefficient to raise the coefficient value above the threshold without affecting the embedded bit and without adding extra noise. In LSBM (± 1) embedding, such a situation occurs when the stego coefficient is obtained by subtraction of 1 from cover coefficient. In this case, if 2 (in general any even number) is added to the stego value, the stego coefficients becomes higher than the threshold. This addition does not change the embedded bit (as addition of even number does not affect the LSB). Again no extra noise is added because still ± 1 embedding is used. To increase steganographic security, the embedding domain is kept secret (i.e. domain separation) such that attackers can not predict the exact embedding domain easily. This domain separation is done here by a novel spatial desynchronization technique called randomized cropping. The algorithm is summarized below:

Algorithm *Steganographic Algorithm with Randomized Cropping (SARC)*
Input: *Cover Image I*
Input Parameters: *threshold value (δ), shared secret seed of PRNG (χ_{PRNG})*
Output: *Stego Image I_S*

1. The cover image I is subject to randomized cropping operation (Ψ) to obtain cropped image I_C.

$$I_C = \Psi(I, \chi_{PRNG}) \tag{1}$$

2. Cropped Image I_C is decomposed into first level wavelet sub-band using integer Wavelet transform.

$$\{I_C^{LL}, I_C^{LH}, I_C^{HL}, I_C^{HH}\} = IntDWT(I_C) \tag{2}$$

where I_C^{LL}, I_C^{LH}, I_C^{HL}, I_C^{HH} are first level LL, LH, HL and HH sub bands in wavelet decomposition of I_C.

3. $I_C^{LH}, I_C^{HL}, I_C^{HH}$ sub-bands are taken for embedding.
4. The coefficients which are greater than the threshold (δ) from each of these sub bands are selected for embedding.
5. Bits are embeded using the LSB matching algorithm with the selected coefficients. When a selected coefficient which is initially above the threshold becomes less than the threshold due to the embedding operation, 2 is added to that stego coefficient to push its value above the threshold without affecting the embedded bit.
6. Continue step 5 loop until all the coefficients are exhausted.
7. After embedding the inverse integer wavelet transform is used to reconstruct the image

$$I_{SC} = Inv\ IntDWT(I_C^{LL}, I_C^{LH'}, I_C^{HL'}, I_C^{HH'}) \tag{3}$$

where LH', HL', HH' are image sub bands after embedding, LL is not used for embedding. I_{SC} is reconstructed cropped version of stego image.

8. Reconstruct the Stego image (I_S) using inverse randomized cropping operation(Ψ_{INV}) on I_{SC}.

$$I_S = \Psi_{INV}(I_{SC}, \chi_{PRNG}) \tag{4}$$

End *Steganographic Algorithm with Randomized Cropping (SARC)*

3.2   Extraction Scheme

Extraction process is quite straight forward. Using the shared secret seed of the pseudorandom number generator (χ_{PRNG}), the cropped version of the stego image is obtained. Then the LH, HL and HH sub bands are determined using integer wavelet transformation same as encoder side. Secret bits are then extracted using standard LSB matching extraction algorithm considering the same local adaptive criterion as the encoder side.

4   Experimental Results

4.1   Embedding Capacity

In Table 2, we have listed the embedding rate (ER) in bpp (bit per pixel) and the corresponding $PSNR$ (psnr) for several standard images using $SARC$ algorithm. δ denotes a predefined threshold value considering as local adaptive criterion. Coefficients, greater than the threshold value, are used for embedding. It can be observed from Table 2 that the PSNR of the stego images with respect to the cover image strictly decreases with decrease of the threshold value (δ) and there is no significant drop in PSNR even after embedding a significant amount of payload.

Table 2. Embedding Rate and Corresponding PSNR of Some Standard Images at Different Values of Thresholds δ

Threshold	Embedding Rate (bpp) and PSNR (dB) for Standard Images														
(δ)	Peppers		Lena		Crowd		Goldhill		airplane		man		boats		harbour	
	ER	psnr	ER	psnr	ER	psnr	ER	psnr	ER	psnr	ER	psnr	ER	psnr	ER	psnr
2	0.44	51.5	0.39	51.9	0.34	52.3	0.44	51.3	0.30	52.8	0.42	51.5	0.34	52.5	0.39	51.8
4	0.29	53.2	0.25	53.7	0.25	53.5	0.31	52.6	0.19	54.7	0.29	52.8	0.22	54.2	0.30	52.8
8	0.15	56.2	0.12	56.7	0.15	55.5	0.16	55.4	0.10	57.2	0.16	55.2	0.11	56.7	0.20	54.2
16	0.05	60.8	0.04	60.8	0.07	58.7	0.05	59.9	0.06	60.2	0.07	58.6	0.05	60.9	0.12	56.5

4.2 Security against Steganalytic Attacks in Comparison with Existing Schemes

The steganographic security of proposed scheme is evaluated against state of art spatial domain blind attacks as well as targeted attacks especially suitable for LSB Matching scheme. For the performance evaluation of the steganographic security, Wavelet Absolute Moment Steganalysis [2], Moulin et al's blind attack based on CF (Characteristic Function) moments [3], Jun Zhang et al 's targeted attack [4] and Fangjun Huang et al 's targeted attack [5] have been used.

For testing the performance of the $SARC$ algorithm, we have used 1000 cover images from an uncompressed image database, UCID [7] and generated 1000 stego images with proposed algorithm. For comparison with $LSBM$ another set of 1000 stego images are generated using $LSBM$ embedding scheme from same set of 1000 cover images. All the images in UCID are high resolution TIFF files with the size 512×384 or 384×512 and appear to be cut from a variety of uncompressed digital camera images. In these experiments, the embedding algorithm is tuned such a way that it terminates when a prescribed payload has been achieved. The threshold (δ) is adaptively set to accommodate it. In LSB matching also, same payload is achieved to all 1000 images. Before testing, the images were converted to grayscale images. Detection accuracy (P_{detect}) [6] which is computed using equations 5 and 6 respectively have been used as the evaluation metric.

$$P_{detect} = 1 - P_{error} \tag{5}$$

$$P_{error} = \frac{1}{2} \times P_{FP} + \frac{1}{2} \times P_{FN} \tag{6}$$

where P_{FP}, P_{FN} are the probabilities of false positive and false negative respectively. A value of $P_{detect} = 0.5$ shows that the classification is as good as random guessing and $P_{detect} = 1.0$ shows a classification with 100% accuracy.

The detection performance (P_{detect}) of the proposed scheme against different targeted and blind attack is presented in the Figure 3. From Figure 3, it can be observed that proposed SARC scheme is almost undetectable (since P_{detect}s are very close to 0.5) against the steganalytic attacks under consideration. The comparison of proposed $SARC$ algorithm with simple LSB matching algorithm ($LSBM$) has been presented in Figures 4 and 5. From these figures, it can be easily seen that for any embedding rate, the detection accuracy (P_{detect}) of the proposed scheme is consistently much lower than that of simple LSBM scheme against both targeted and blind attacks. Since $SARC$ is basically LSB matching algorithm wrapped with proposed scheme, then it can be concluded that proposed scheme has increased the stagnographic security of LSB matching algorithm. Furthermore, the proposed scheme can be easily incorporated with any other LSB matching type steganographic algorithms to increase its security.

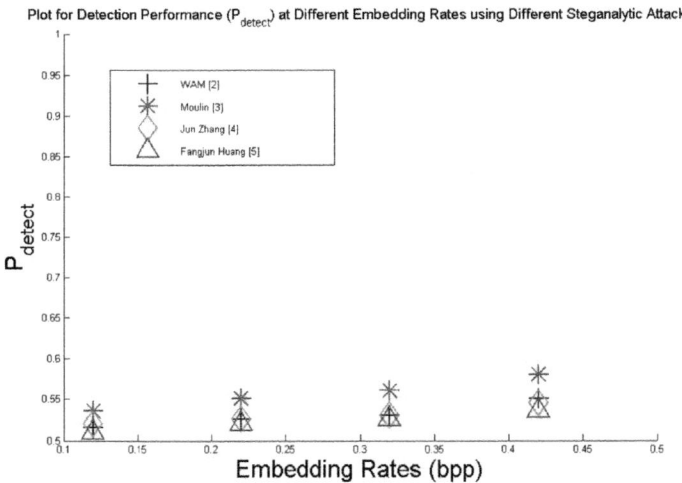

Fig. 3. Detectability of the Proposed SARC Scheme against Different Steganlysis

4.3   Effect of Randomized Cropping on Steganalytic Detection

One of the main contributions of the proposed scheme is the concept of randomized cropping which is used to separate out the embedding domain from the steganalytic domain. Now in the proposed algorithm there are two main issues; firstly the cover image I is subject to randomized cropping operation (Ψ) to obtain the cropped image I_C and secondly, first level integer wavelet coefficients are used for embedding the secret bits. This raises a question that which of these two operations makes the scheme more secure. A brief experiment is presented in this subsection to answer this question. In this experiment, we compare the performance of the proposed scheme against the proposed scheme without randomized cropping operation. In second algorithm, secrets bits are embedded in

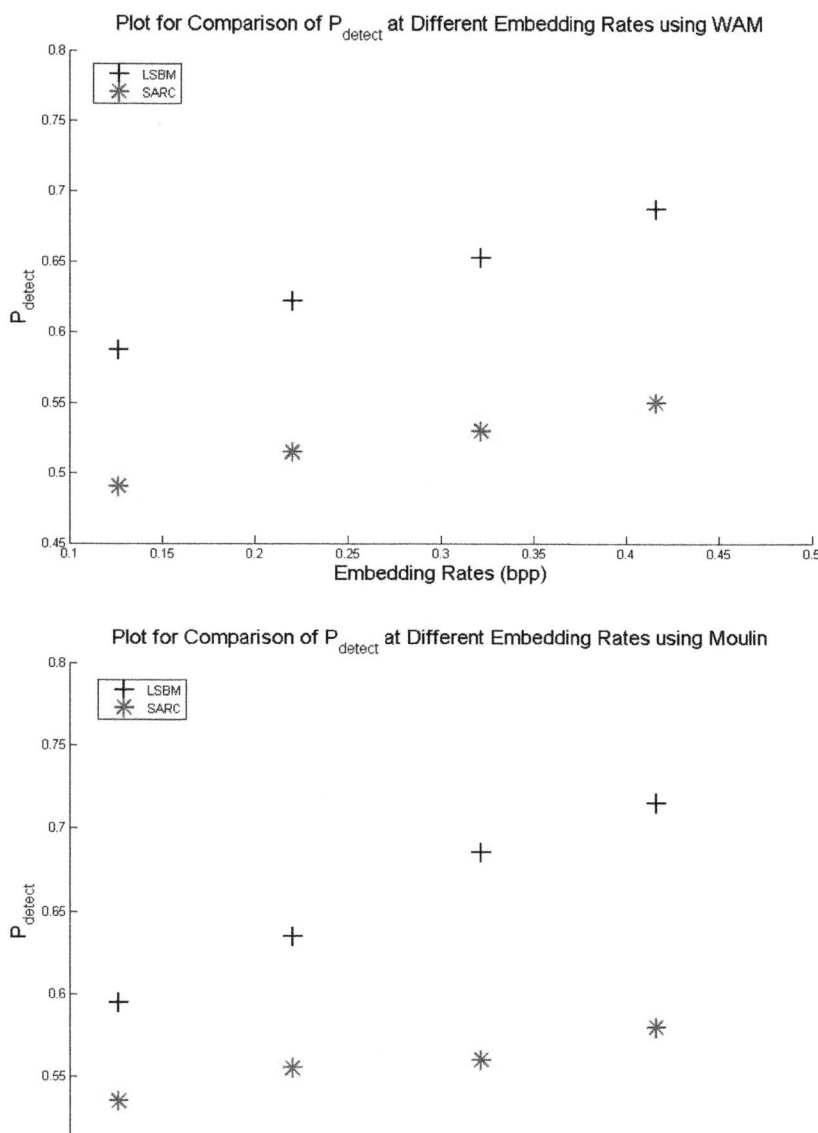

Fig. 4. Comparison of Detectability (P_{detect}) against WAM and Moulin et al 's Blind attacks

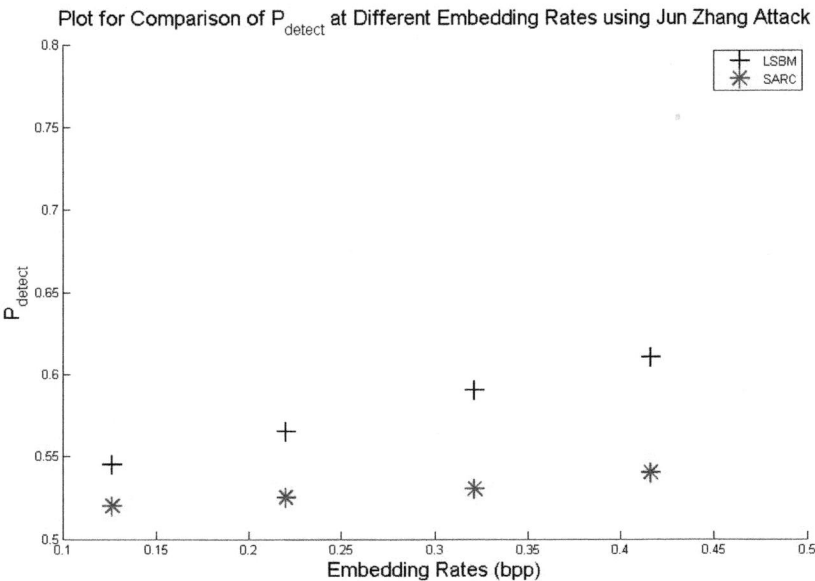

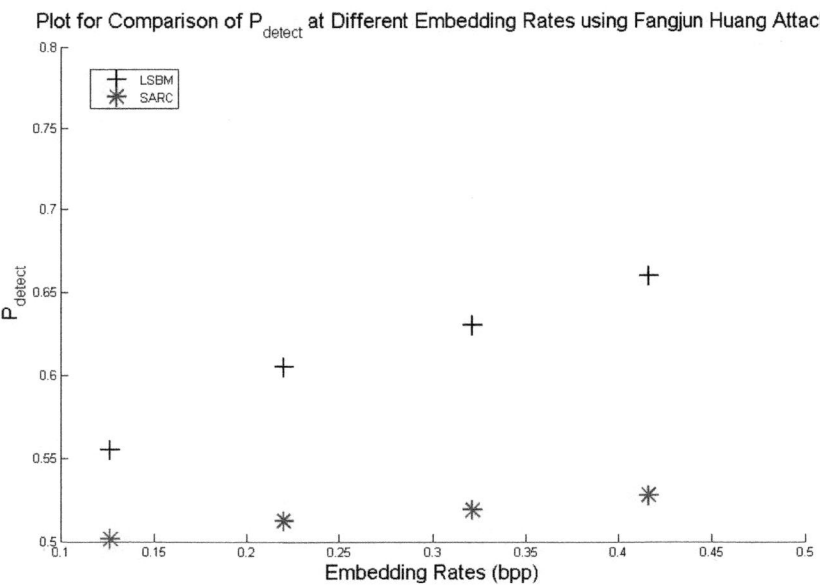

Fig. 5. Comparison of Detectability (P_{detect}) against Jun Zhang et al 's and Fangjun Huang et al 's targeted attacks

the integer wavelet domain but the cover images do not subject to the randomized cropping operation initially. WAM [2] has been used as the steganalytic attack. The comparison of detection performance of these two cases are given in the Figure 6.

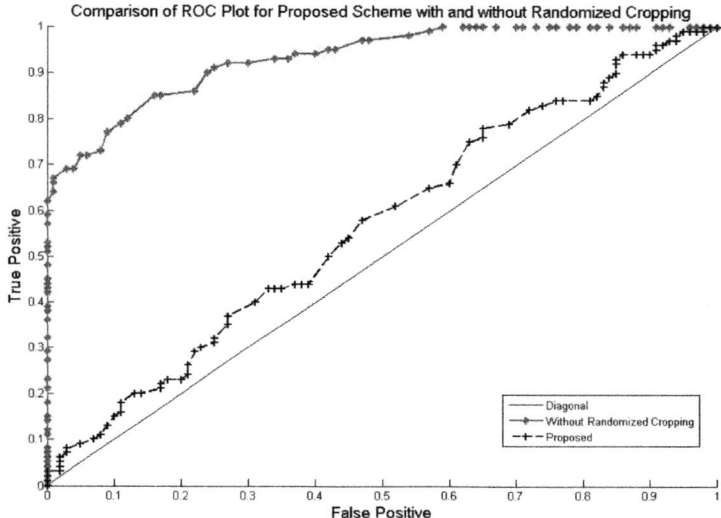

Fig. 6. Comparison of ROC Plot for Proposed Scheme with and without Randomized Cropping

It can be observed from the Figure 6 that if secret bits are only embedding in the integer wavelet domain without randomized cropping operation, the scheme is more readily detectable against blind steganalytic attack. Here, it is noted that the embedding domain and steganalytic domain are same which is not true for the proposed $SARC$ algorithm. This observation implies that randomized cropping operation makes the scheme more secure by separating the embedding domain from steganalytic domain. In other words, proposed randomized cropping operation hides the embedding domain itself from the attacker by randomizing it.

4.4   Effect of Different Cropping Dimensions on Steganalytic Detection

As discussed in Sec. 2.2, in our experiments for randomized cropping operation, two rows and two columns have been randomly cropped (say the cropping dimension is m = 2 and n = 2) for experiments. It is an interesting study that how the steganalytic detection is varying with the change of the cropping dimension (no. of rows and columns to be cropped). A small experiment has been carried out where different cropping dimension (for example m=2,n=2; m=16,n=16 and m=64,n=64) are used for a fixed payload. To maintain a fixed payload in different cropping dimension, threshold is varied accordingly. The resulting ROC curves have been presented in Figure 7.

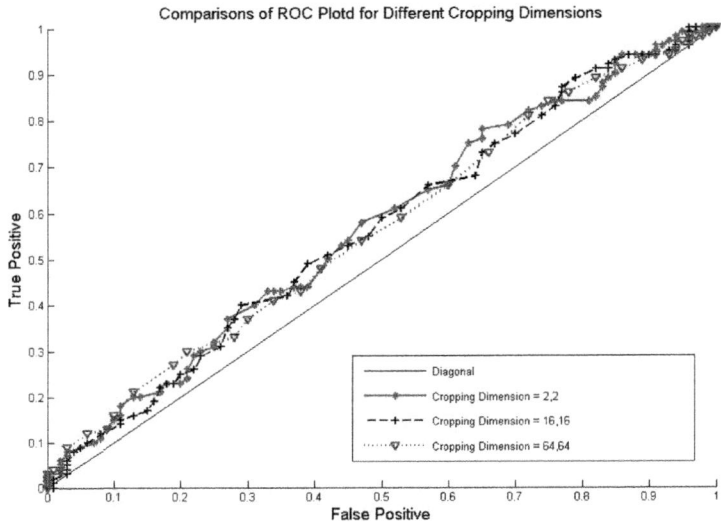

Fig. 7. Comparison of ROC Plot for Different No. of rows and columns are Cropped

It can be observed from the Figure 7 that the detection performance is very comparative for the different cropping dimension. It implies that the chance of detection does not reduced with higher cropping dimension. One intuitive reason is that the embedding space become small if relatively large cropping dimension is used. This makes the embedding density more packed and thus large cropping dimension makes the embedding more detectable. So it can be concluded that although higher cropping dimension may increase the no. of randomized domains, it increases the embedding density for a fixed payload and thus it can not enhanced the overall steganalytic security substantially.

5   Discussion and Conclusion

In this paper, an adaptive steganographic scheme is proposed to increase steganographic security of spatial domain embedding scheme like LSB matching. Data bits are embedded in image regions with high level of high frequency components such that high frequency components mask the steganographic noise. Secondly, the embedding domain is kept secret from attackers using a novel concept called randomized cropping such that effectiveness of steganalytic features gets reduced for blind attacks. Experimental results show that the LSB matching algorithm wrapped with proposed scheme (the *SARC* algorithm) performs considerably better than simple LSB matching embedding algorithm against spatial domain steganalytic attacks. Another notable advantage of the proposed randomized cropping operation is that it can be easily incorporated with any transformed domain schemes based on LSB matching like embedding.

References

1. Chandramouli, R., Kharrazi, M., Memon, N.D.: Image steganography and steganalysis: Concepts and practice. In: Kalker, T., Cox, I., Ro, Y.M. (eds.) IWDW 2003. LNCS, vol. 2939, pp. 35–49. Springer, Heidelberg (2004)
2. Goljan, M., Fridrich, J., Holotyak, T.: New blind steganalysis and its implications. In: Proceedings of SPIE. Security, Steganography, and Watermarking of Multimedia Contents VIII, vol. 6072, pp. 1–13 (January 2006)
3. Wang, Y., Moulin, P.: Optimized feature extraction for learning-based image steganalysis. IEEE Transactions On Information Forensics and Security 2(1), 31–45 (2007)
4. Zhang, J., Cox, I.J., Doerr, G.: Steganalysis for LSB Matching in Images with High-frequency Noise. In: Proc. IEEE 9th Workshop on Multimedia Signal Processing, MMSP 2007, pp. 385–388 (2007)
5. Huang, F., Li, B., Huang, J.: Attack LSB Matching Steganography by Counting Alteration Rate of the Number of Neighbourhood Gray Levels. In: Proc. IEEE International Conference on Image Processing, ICIP 2007, vol. 1, pp. 1401–1404 (2007)
6. Solanki, K., Sarkar, A., Manjunath, B.S.: YASS: Yet Another Steganographic Scheme That Resists Blind Steganalysis. In: Furon, T., Cayre, F., Doërr, G., Bas, P. (eds.) IH 2007. LNCS, vol. 4567, pp. 16–31. Springer, Heidelberg (2008)
7. Schaefer, G., Stich, M.: UCID - An Uncompressed Colour Image Database. In: Proc. SPIE, Storage and Retrieval Methods and Applications for Multimedia, vol. 5307, pp. 472–480 (2004)
8. Dewitte, S., Cornelis, J.: Lossless integer wavelet transform. IEEE Signal Processing Letters 4(6), 158–160 (1997)
9. Sweldens, W.: The Lifting Scheme: a Construction of Second Generation of Wavelets. SIAM J. Math. Anal. 29(2), 511–546 (1998)
10. Chen, B., Wornell, G.W.: Quantization Index Modulation: A Class of Provably Good Methods for Digital Watermarking and Information Embedding. IEEE Transactions on Information Theory 47(4), 1423–1443 (2001)

Steganography in Streaming Multimedia over Networks

Hong Zhao[1], Yun Q. Shi[2], and Nirwan Ansari[2]

[1] Fairleigh Dickinson University, Teaneck, NJ 07666 USA
zhao@fdu.edu
[2] New Jersey Institute of Technology, Newark, NJ 07102 USA
{shi,nirwan.ansari}@njit.edu

Abstract. This paper presents steganography methods to covertly transmit data via RTP (Real-time Transport Protocol) header and RTP payload in multimedia streaming over networks. The proposed covert channels do not change the original traffic pattern. The bandwidth and the impact of the proposed covert channels on the received video quality are analyzed. Steganalysis of the proposed hiding methods is also discussed and the proposed covert channels cannot be detected by traffic pattern, received video quality, or the statistical property required by the standard. Simulations on real video traces and RTP packets collected from multicasting videos to LAN (Local Area Network) are conducted and the results show the proposed covert channels not only achieve relatively high bandwidth but also keep the received video quality high or unchanged. Those features make the proposed covert channels practical and not easy to be detected.

Keywords: Network steganography, information hiding, covert channels.

1 Introduction

Steganography is the art and science of writing hidden message to a cover medium in such a way that no one except the sender and intended recipient, suspects the existence of the message. The most widely used cover media include images, sound and video files. Hiding data at network level such as protocols and timing control of arrived packets is relatively new but it becomes an important issue for network security. All information hiding techniques that may be used to exchange stego-data in telecommunications networks can be classified under general term of network steganography [1]. As secret message gets passed via users' normal data transmissions in a completely undetectable manner, we also refer this communication channel as covert channel. The covert channel must be contained within a transport medium rather than within a static medium and therefore in transport. Thus, the covert channel would acquire a fleeting property in that if not captured, it cannot be proven that the covert channel ever existed [2]. Traditionally, covert channels were classified into storage and timing channels. A storage covert channel involves a storage location to which the covert

Y.Q. Shi (Ed.): Transactions on DHMS VII, LNCS 7110, pp. 96–114, 2012.

channel sender writes and from which the receiver reads, usually indirectly. A timing covert channel is established when the sender modulates the receiver's observed response time in a way that can provide information. Covert channels can be used by government agencies to keep their communications secret as simply using encryption does not prevent adversaries from detecting communication patterns. Most of time, only the evidence that communication takes place is sufficient to detect the ongoing activity [3]. Hiding secret data in normal data transmission would be a candidate for this purpose. Network administrators can use covert channels to secure network management related communications by hiding it from hackers[4]. Covert channels can also be used for transmitting authentication data, which allows authorized external users to access open firewall ports while presenting these ports as closed to all other users. In [5] the authors present a technique called "port knocking" which uses covert channels to send authentication information.

The performance of covert channels is evaluated based on bandwidth, reliability and undetectability. The bandwidth or capacity is defined by how much data can be inserted in cover media. Reliability talks about impact on normal communications by introducing covert channels. Undetectability deals with steganalysis which is to identify suspected information stream, determine whether or not they have stego-data hidden in them and if possible recover the stego-data.

Multimedia consists of voice, video, and data. Streaming multimedia is multimedia that is constantly received by and presented to an end-user while being delivered by a streaming provider. It is usually applied to media that are distributed over telecommunication networks. Sample applications of multimedia streaming include video conference, video on demand, distance learning, and movies on demand. Multimedia streaming becomes the major traffic over networks and huge volume of data make it an ideal candidate for covert communications. Hiding data in audio has been addressed in [6] through different codecs, and even in VoIP. However, some of them are just theory papers and do not explain how they intend to accomplish certain tasks. In [7], Mazurczyk and Szczpiorski proposed hiding data in signalling protocol SIP (Session Initiation Protocol) for VoIP (Voice over IP) service. In it, the authors evaluate available steganographic techniques for SIP that can be used for creating covert channels during signalling phase of VoIP call. Mazurczyk and Lubacz[8] also proposed using lost audio packets to embed secret data in VoIP streams, called LACK (Lost Audio PaCKets Steganography). The hidden data insertion rate was analyzed based on call duration probability distributions, and this insertion rate is dependent on the call duration distribution. The implementation of LACK is complex and its effectiveness depends on the accuracy of the estimated mean call duration and the coefficient of variation of the call duration. Furthermore, the impact of the LACK on quality of the received voice was not analyzed, which is an important feature for covert channel. If the received voice quality is deteriorated, the covert channel can be easily noticed and thus it is not practical. All these hiding methods are for VoIP service. To the author's best knowledge hiding data based on multimedia streaming service has not been addressed. In this paper, two types of covert channel are proposed. One is using RTP header and the other one is using RTP payload when streaming multimedia over networks. The proposed hidden channel using RTP payload of MPEG-2 (Moving Picture Experts Group) videos covertly transmits data through either delayed B frame packets or normal B frame packets via multimedia steaming over networks. The proposed hidden channel in RTP header uses Sequence Number (SEQ) and SSRC (Synchronization Source Identifer) which allow for modification of them to create covert channels. The stego_SSRC and stego_SEQ which have hidden messages in it, are compared with normal SSRC and SEQ, and they have the same statistical property. Thus, it is hard to be detected. For covert channel using RTP payload, the bandwidth of the covert channels, the impact on the received video quality are analyzed quantitatively. We also discuss the detectability of these proposed covert channels. Simulations on real MPEG-2 video traces are conducted and results show that the proposed covert channels not only achieve relatively high bandwidth but also keep the received video quality high, which makes it practical and not easy to be detected. The implementation complexity is compared with LACK and our proposed method is simpler. No statistical analysis is required in implementation. The rest of the paper is organized as follows: Section 2 briefly introduces the Transport Streams (TS) of MPEG-2 videos and the packetizing the TS streams into RTP packets. The proposed hidden channels are presented in Section 3 and 4. Simulations and performance analysis on capacity, detectability of the proposed covert channels, and the impact on the received video quality are presented in Section 5. Finally concluding remarks are given in Section 6.

2   Packetization of MPEG-2 Video Frames into RTP Packets

MPEG-2 is widely used standard for video compression. It takes advantage of temporal and spacial redundancy to reduce the number of bits in each frame and generates I, B and P frames accordingly. Among those frames I frames are intra-coded which contain full picture information; P frames are inter-coded frames which are predicted from past I or P frames; B frames are bi-directional frames which use past and future I or P frames for motion compensation. The different types of pictures typically occur in a repeating sequence, termed Group of Pictures (GOP). A typical GOP in display order is $I_1B_2B_3P_4B_5B_6P_7B_8B_9P_{10}B_{11}B_{12}$. A regular GOP structure can be described with two parameters: N which is the number of pictures in the GOP and M which is the spacing of P-pictures. The given example here is described as $N = 12$ and $M = 3$. For a given decoded picture quality, coding using each picture type produces different number of bits. In a typical example sequence, a coded I frame was three times larger than a coded P frame, which was itself 50 percent larger than a coded B frame. When transmitting videos over networks, in order for a decoder at receiver side to reconstruct a B-frame from the preceding I and following P-frames, both I and P frames must arrive first. So the order of frame transmission must be different from the order of frame display. For the above example the transmission order is $I_1 P_4 B_2 B_3 P_7 B_5 B_6 P_{10} B_8 B_9 I_{13} B_{11} B_{12}$. But for this to work, the decoder must know at what time it should show the frames which is their order in time. The related control information such as DTS (Decode Time Stamp), PTS (Presentation Time Stamp) are added to each frame to form the Packetized Elementary Stream (PES). A PES packet is then broken into TS packets which is of 188 bytes including 4 bytes of control information to form TS to be transmitted over networks [9]. Fig. 1 shows the construction of TS from video elementary stream.

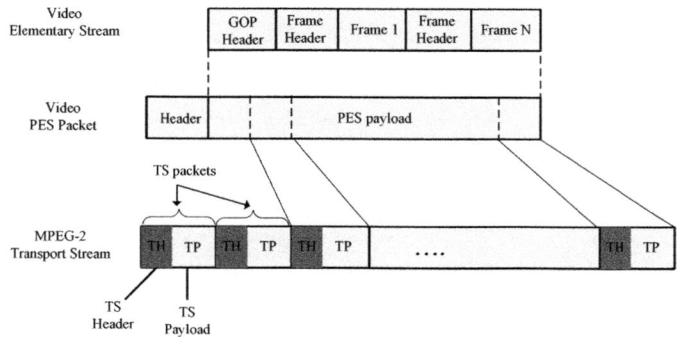

Fig. 1. The construction MPEG-2 transport stream from video elementary stream

There are two methods currently utilized for the carriage of TS packets over IP (Internet Protocol). The first simply selects a number of TS packets and carries them as payload of the UDP (User Datagram Protocol) datagram. The second method specified by the IETF RFC2250 [10] uses RTP to carry TS packets. In this case, the RTP payload again carries an integral number of TS packets. For Ethernet based networks with a Maximum Transmission Unit (MTU) of 1500 bytes, the payload for RTP would be $1500/188 = 7$ packets [11]. In both of these two methods sequential TS packets are carried in the payload without any specific knowledge about the content of the packets. RTP is a transport protocol for real-time applications and it provides support for applications with real-time properties such as continuous media [11]. It has support of numerous error resilience mechanism that are well suited for transporting videos over IP networks. The reception quality feedback is standardized by RTCP (RTP Control Protocol) and QoS (Quality of Service) could be provided. Given the multiple advantages of using RTP, we adopt the second method–that is to use RTP to carry TS packets to transport MPEG-2 videos over Internet. The following Fig. 2 shows that in multimedia streaming, video data is carried in an RTP packet carried in a UDP packet carried in an IP packet. To make an RTP payload the RFC2250 [10] suggests the following rules:

- The MPEG Video_Sequence_Header, when present, will always be at the beginning of an RTP payload.

- An MPEG GOP_Header, when present, will always be at the beginning of the RTP payload, or will follow a video sequence header.
- An MPEG Picture_Header, when present, will always be at the beginning of a RTP payload, or will follow a GOP_Header.

Based on the above rules, we propose to packetize a B-frame in one RTP packet and any frame larger than the biggest B frame would be broken into several RTP packets.

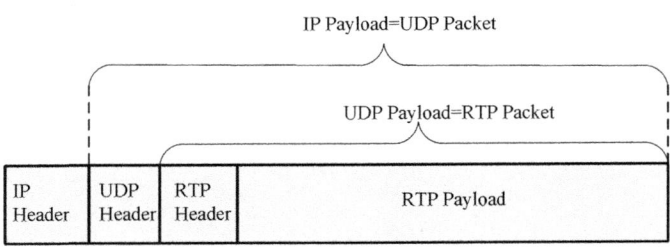

Fig. 2. The RTP packet payload format

3   The Proposed Hidden Channels in RTP Header

In Section 2, we talked about how MPEG-2 videos are packetized into IP packets, and RTP is used to carry MPEG-2 TS packets over networks instead of putting TS packets directly into UDP payload. RTP brings several advantages over TS when transmitting real-time videos such as better error resilience, improved efficiency, and improved services. More importantly, it has good integration with other internet protocols and it makes use of an associated protocol, the RTCP, which provides quality of service monitoring and information used to synchronize multiple RTP streams. RTP together with RTCP protocols provide controlled delivery of multimedia traffic over the Internet. To better understand how RTP works and how to create covert channels in RTP, let us look at the RTP header fields and functions provided by those header fields. Fig. 3 shows the RTP header structure and the explanation of the corresponding entity is illustrated in Table 1.

For the MPEG-2 TS encapsulation, the RTP fixed header fields are used as follows:

- Payload Type: Distinct payload types should be assigned for video elementary streams and audio elementary streams. For the use of MPEG-2 TS, the value 33 is assigned.
- M bit: Set to 1 whenever the timestamp is discontinuous. This allows the receiver and any intervening RTP mixers or translators that are synchronizing to the flow to ignore the difference between this timestamp and any previous timestamp in their clock phase detector.

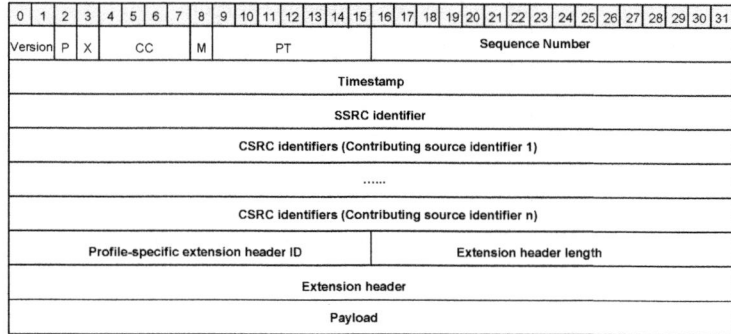

Fig. 3. The RTP header format

- Timestamp: 32-bit 90kHz timestamp representing presentation time of MPEG-2 picture. Same for all packets that make up a picture. May not be monotonically increasing in video stream if B pictures present in stream.

The use of other fields is explained in Table 1. Covert channels in RTP exploit the fact that some headers could be altered to carry information in transit without impacting normal communications. An analysis of the areas of a typical RTP header that are either unused or optional reveals many possibilities where data can be stored or transmitted. In Fig. 3, padding field may be needed by some encryption algorithms. If the padding bit is set, the packet contains one or more additional padding octets at the end of header which are not part of the payload. The number of data that can be added after the header is defined in last octet of the padding as it contains a count of how many padding octets should be ignored. By using those additional padding octets, secret information could be carried on [13]. The extension header has the similar situation as the padding mechanism. When the X bit is set, a variable length header extension may be used to hide secret message. The least significant bit of Timestamp field can be utilized in a similar way as proposed covert channel in TCP (Transport Control Protocol) Timestamp field in [14] because lower bits in Timestamp field are random. These covert channels which use the unused header fields or modify some header fields could be easily detected through implementation of an automated mechanism to only monitor such fields. For example, if the padding field is 0, it means that there will be no padding octet at the end of header and then covert message could be embedded there. In this case the network could simply monitor the P field and clear the padding octet at the end of header if the padding field P is not set, then the hidden information will be destroyed. However, hidden data in the Sequence Number (SEQ) and SSRC cannot be detected easily as those two fields require to hold random data. In this paper, SEQ (16-bit) and SSRC (32-bit) will be manipulated to carry ASCII values of the secret message for transmission to the intended recipient.

The 16-bit SEQ is used by the receiver to detect packet loss and to restore packet sequence. It is incremented by one for each RTP data packet. RTP

Table 1. RTP header illustration

Version	Indicates the version of the protocol.
P-Padding	Used to indicate if there are extra padding bytes at the end of the RTP packet.
X-Extension	Indicates presence of an extension header.
CC-CSRC Count	Contains the number of CSRC.
M-Marker	Used at the application level. If it is set, it means that the current data has some special relevance for the application.
PT-Payload Type	Indicates which codec is used to encode the payload.
Sequence Number	The sequence number is incremented by one for each RTP data packet. The initial value of the sequence number is random.
Timestamp	Used to enable the receiver to play back the received samples at appropriate intervals.
SSRC	Synchronization source identifier uniquely identifies the source of a stream. This identifier is chosen randomly, with the intent that no two synchronization sources within the same RTP session will have the same SSRC identifier.
CSRC: (0 to 15 items, 32-bit each)	The CSRC list identifies the contributing sources for the payload contained in this packet. The number of identifiers is given by the CC field.
Extension Header (Optional)	The first 32-bit contains a profile-specific identifier (16-bit) and the length the extension.

provides no guarantee of delivery, but the presence of SEQs makes it possible to detect missing packets. According to RFC 3550[15], the initial value of SEQ should be random to make known-plain text attacks on encryption more difficult. The sequence number of the first RTP packet can be utilized for covert communication. As RTP is designed to support multicast transmission, RTP packet includes a SSRC which identifies the source of a stream. There are two types of sources: a mixer and a translator. Translators forward packets with SSRC identifiers intact; mixers combine packets from multiple senders and forward them to one or more destinations. The mixer assigns itself as the sender of the packet and generates a SSRC for the combined packet. The identifiers of all contributing sources (CSRC) are attached to the combined RTP packet. The example of mixers and translators from [16] is shown in Fig. 4. In it, the mixer M1 combines packets from S1 and S2 and assigns a new SSRC 48 to the combined packet. The identifiers $(1, 17)$ become contributing sources and are attached to the combined packet. The translators T1 and T2 forward packets with SSRC identifiers intact such as packets $48(1, 17), 89(64, 65)$ handled by T2. The SSRC identifiers SHOULD be chosen randomly, with the intent that no two synchronization sources within the same RTP session will have the same SSRC identifier. In Fig. 4, all SSRC identifiers, whether from mixers or senders, are different. This makes the 32-bit SSRC a candidate for covert communication.

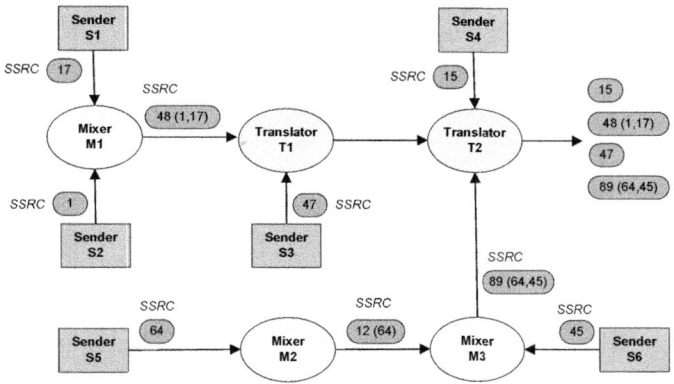

Fig. 4. Mixers and Translators example [16]

Therefore, we will encode and decode the SEQ and SSRC fields in RTP header. The basis of the exploitation relies on encoding ASCII values of the range $0-127$ into lower 8-bit of these two fields. The modified SSRCs and SEQs still look random. By using this method it is possible to pass text messages between two hosts in packets that appear to be initial packets, or the regular packets. These packets contain actual MPEG-2 videos. The proposed method simply replaces the least 8-bit of SSRC or SEQ with actual ASCII code used in the text message. The intended receiver reads the least 8-bit of SSRC or SEQ fields to get the text message. Fig. 5 shows the embedding process. This embedding method allows for easy covert transmission and fast embedding speed. As the stego-data is embedded in the lower 8-bit of SSRC and SEQ fields, it has little impact on the randomness required by these two fields. Simulation results are presented in section 5.1.

4   The Proposed Hidden Channels in RTP Payload

In multimedia streaming over networks, packets are sent in decoding order. For the example given in Section II, the decoding order is $I_1 P_4 B_2 B_3 P_7 B_5 B_6 P_{10} B_8 B_9 I_{13} B_{11} B_{12}$. When packet loss occurs, it can lead to decoding errors in one or more of these frame types on the receiving end of video frames. Errors in I or P frames will propagate through the remaining B and P frames within a GOP. An error in a B frame, however does not propagate to subsequent frames and may not even noticeable to the viewer. The Fig 6 shows the damage in B frames has the least impact on the overall video quality. Thus, B frames are selected as candidates for carrying stego-data. we propose the following two covert channels in multimedia streaming.

- Replace the RTP packets of B frame payload and transmit these packets as normal packets.

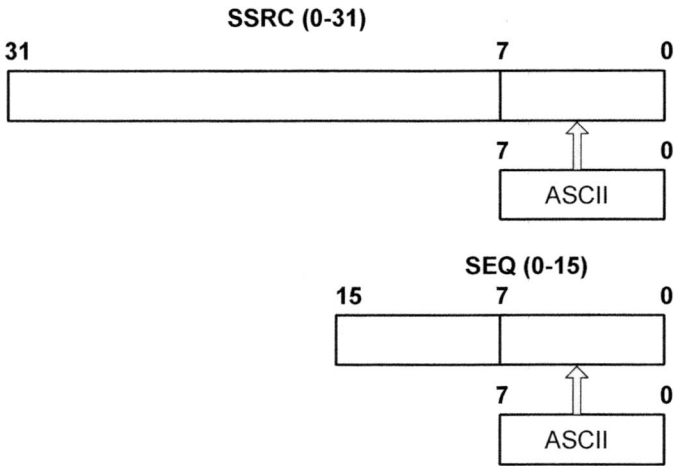

Encoding ASCII in SSRC and SEQ fields

Fig. 5. Embedding ASCII code of text message in SSRC and SEQ fields of RTP header

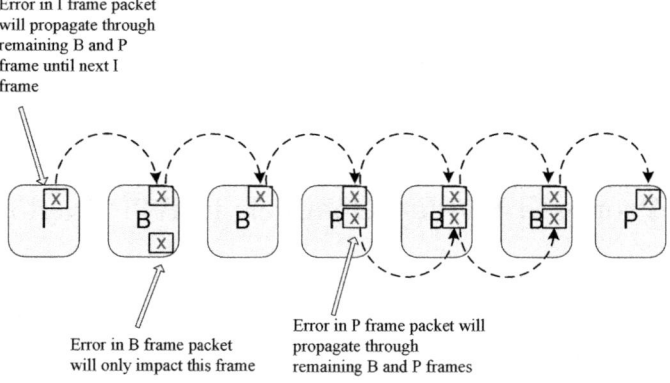

Fig. 6. The impact of frame loss on video quality

– Replace the RTP packets of B frame payload and delay the transmission of these packets intentionally.

Both delayed and normal transmitted B frame packets with payload replaced are considered lost packets and will be dropped at the receiver side. This is because the delayed packets missed their display times and the normal B frame packets with payload contents replaced with stego-data do not have the corresponding control information. As a result they will be dropped at the receiver side. The lost packets will cause the video quality be deteriorated. Thus acceptable level of packet loss for video streaming must be controlled in this stegangrophy procedure. In considering the possible hidden communication scenarios, there are 6 possible hidden channels[17] as shown in Fig 7.

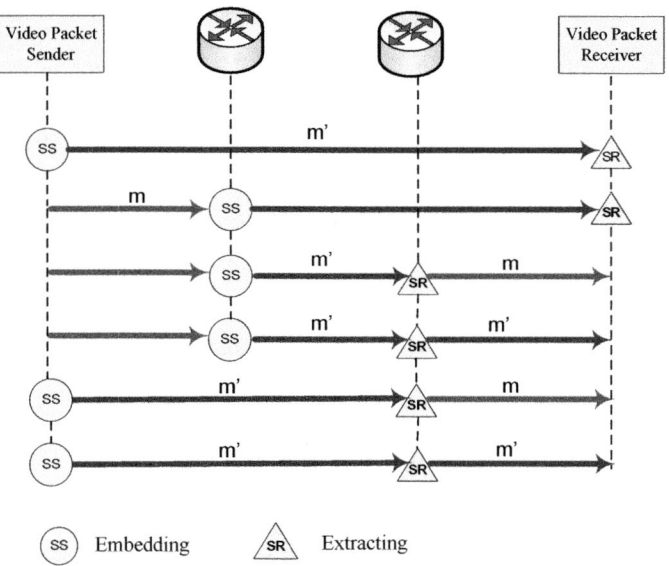

Fig. 7. Possible hidden channels in a communication system

Among those six possible hidden channels. The secret message could be inserted at the sender side or at the intermediate routers; the third party which is to receive the secret message could be at the receiver side or the intermediate routers. In Fig. 7 m represents the original packet and m' represents stego-message packets which contains hidden information in it. After receiving the m', the stego-message receiver could simply drop it or resend it to the video packet receiver. The proposed two covert channels can be used in any one of the six possible hidden communication channels. To guarantee a certain level of video quality at the video packet receiver, we need consider how many B frame packets can be used in carrying stego-message. On the other hand if the video quality deteriorates due to the embedding secret data, the covert channel would be identified easily. Thus, maintaining certain level of video quality must be considered in designing covert channels via multimedia streaming.

There are several ways to estimate video quality including both objective testing and subjective testing. Subjective testing is a traditional, well proven method of evaluating video quality that provides good results; however, it can be very expensive, time consuming, and impractical for many applications. Objective testing methods use objective test metrics to calculate estimated video quality scores. In this paper we use the most widely used full reference algorithm PSNR (Peak Signal-to-Noise Ratio) to estimate the received video quality which is considered objective test metrics. PSNR measures the mean error between input and output as a ratio of the peak signal level expressed in dB. The PSNR is defined as follows:

$$PSNR = 10 \cdot log_{10} \frac{p^2}{MSE}, \tag{1}$$

where p denotes the maximum luminance value of a pixel (255 in 8-bit pictures). Since people are more sensitive to luminance information than chrominance; here we only consider PSNR of luminance. The MSE (Mean Square Error) for an individual video frame n is defined as:

$$M_n = \frac{1}{D_x \cdot D_y} \sum_{x=1}^{D_x} \sum_{x=1}^{D_y} [I(n, x, y) - \bar{I}(n, x, y)]^2. \tag{2}$$

$I(n, x, y), n = 0, 1, \ldots, N - 1, x = 1, \ldots, D_x, y = 1, \ldots, D_y$, denotes the luminance value of the pixel at (x, y) of the nth frame in the video sequence with N frames. The mean MSE for a video sequence of N video frames is

$$\bar{M} = \frac{1}{N} \sum_{n=0}^{N-1} M_n. \tag{3}$$

A PSNR value of $35dB$ is generally considered "good", with values below $20dB$ considered unacceptable. The PSNR is used in our simulations to evaluate the received video quality.

5   Performance Analysis and Simulation Results

Simulations on two proposed hiding methods are conducted through collected RTP packets and MPEG-2 videos provided by [18]. The detailed experiment settings and simulation results are presented in subsections 5.1 and 5.2, respectively.

5.1   Experimental Results of Hiding Data in SSRC and SEQ Fields of RTP

The experiment was carried out within ConferenceXP, which is an open source platform for real-time collaboration. ConferenceXP provides simple, flexible, and

Table 2. Statistical characteristics of normal SSRC and stego_SSRC

	Mean (10^9)	Maximum (10^9)	Minimum	Stdev (10^9)
Normal SSRC	1.749307335834	4.291357133	769672	1.192106416
Stego_ SSRC	1.749307254256	4.291357015	769580	1.192106411

Table 3. Statistical characteristics of normal SEQ and stego_SSEQ

	Mean	Maximum	Minimum	Stdev
Normal SEQ	32908	65470	309	18727
Stego_SEQ	32838	65392	282	18728

extensible video conferencing and collaboration using high-bandwidth networks and the advanced multimedia capabilities of Microsoft Windows. A software named RTP_Broadcasting is written based on ConferenceXP. This software multicast videos to a group of users. An multicast IP address 224.0.0.1 is assigned to this group. Any user who joins this multicast group can receive the videos sent by the RTP_Broadcasting. In this software, MSR.LST.NET.Rtp.dll is used to implement the function of generating RTP packets. These RTP packets are then wrapped in UDP followed by IP which will be created by operating system. In our experiment, Windows 7 operating system is used. To collect normal SSRC and SEQ, software WireShark [19] is used to capture RTP packets. Wireshark is the world's foremost network protocol analyzer. It lets you capture and interactively browse the traffic running on a computer network. In our experiment, a filter is added to WireShark to capture the packets we want. The filter is set: ip.addr= 224.0.0.1 and decode UDP stream as RTP. By doing this we could collect the RTP packets sent by RTP_Broadcasting and then extract the SSRCs and SEQs. These are normal SSRCs and SEQs. To embed secret messages, the least 8-bit of collected SSRC or SEQ are replaced by ASCII code of the secret message. The newly formed SSRC or SEQ are called stego_SSRC or stego_SEQ which contain secret information. In our simulation, the secret message is generated randomly and contains all possible ASCII codes $(0 - 127)$. We compared normal SSRC with stego_SSRC and the statistical property of these two sequences are almost the same. Fig 8 shows normalized SSRC and stego_SSRC. Note that, they all show randomness. Table 2 presents the statistical information. In Table 2 both SSRC and stego_SSRC have almost the same mean, maximum, minimum and standard deviation values. The comparison of SEQ and stego_SEQ is shown in Fig. 9, and the corresponding statistical information is presented in Table 3. Both SEQ and stego_SEQ have the same statistical information and it is hard to identify stego_SEQ. Steganalysis to the proposed covert channel using SSRC or SEQ is difficult as both stego_SSRC and stego_SEQ show the randomness as the regular SSRC and SEQ do. The proposed covert channel has no impact on video quality as the payload of RTP packet is not touched, and there is no change in traffic pattern. The covert channel cannot be detected based on the received video quality, or the traffic pattern.

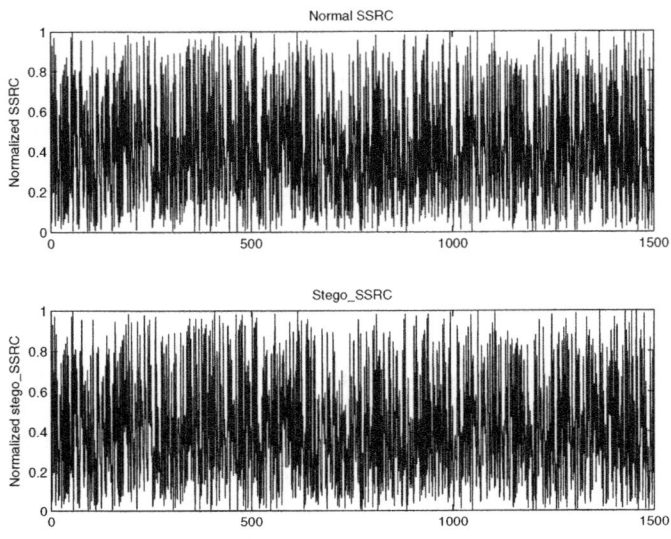

Fig. 8. Comparison of Normal SSRC with stego_SSRC

5.2   Experimental Results of Hiding Data in RTP Payload

An MPEG-2 video sequence *Terminator 2* which is 10 minutes long with GOP of 12 is used in our simulations [20]. The PSNR is used in evaluating the video quality. The average PSNR of *Terminator 2* before transmission is 40.18 dB. The average data rate for this piece of video is 3.22 Mbit/s. To guarantee the received video quality, the number of B frames used in carrying steganographic data should be controlled. In the following simulations we first consider to insert steganorgraphic data or secret data in the first B frames for every GOP. At the receiver side, the stego_B packets will be discarded by a receiver which is not aware of steganography procedure. For the receiver which knows about the steganography procedure, the stego_message will be extracted from those packets. The performance will be evaluated in terms of the received video quality and the bandwidth of covert channel. The simulation shows the capacity of hidden channel is 199.4 kbit/s and the average PSNR of the received video is 36.83 dB, which is still considered good quality. If we decrease the hidden data insertion rate, which is to use the first B frames in every two GOPs or three GOPs, the video quality could be increased. Fig. 10 shows the received video quality versus insertion rate–which is measured in the number of GOP used as a cycle to insert stego_message.

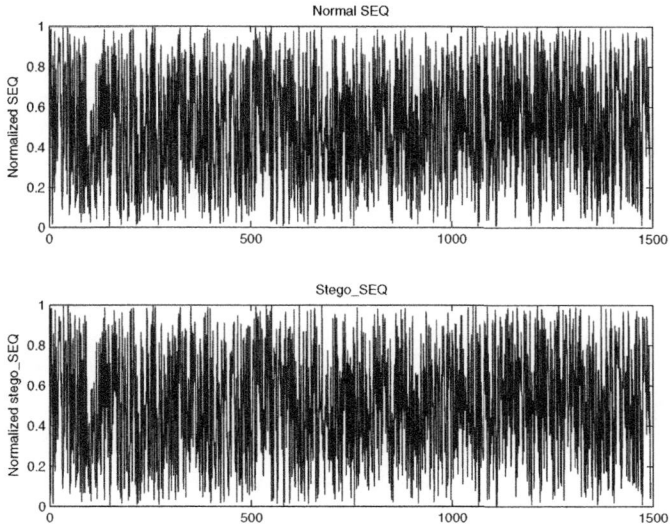

Fig. 9. Comparison of Normal SEQ with stego_SEQ

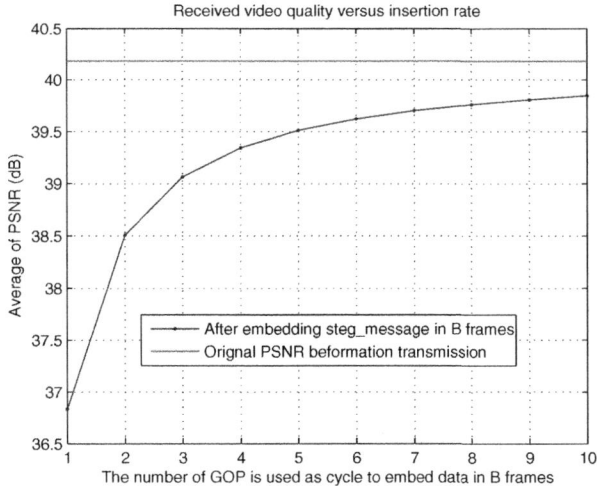

Fig. 10. Received average video quality at different insertion rate

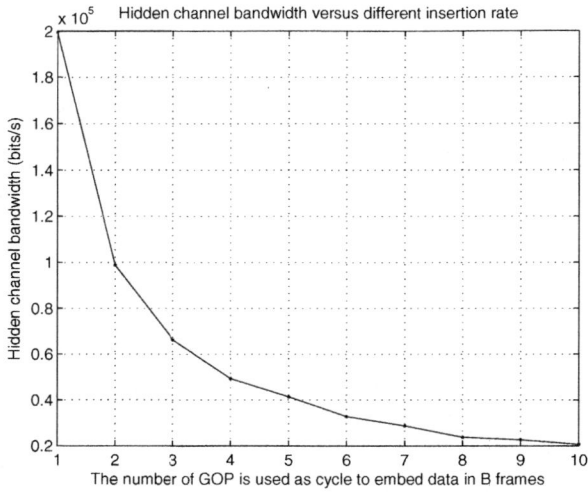

Fig. 11. Hidden channel bandwidth versus different insertion rates

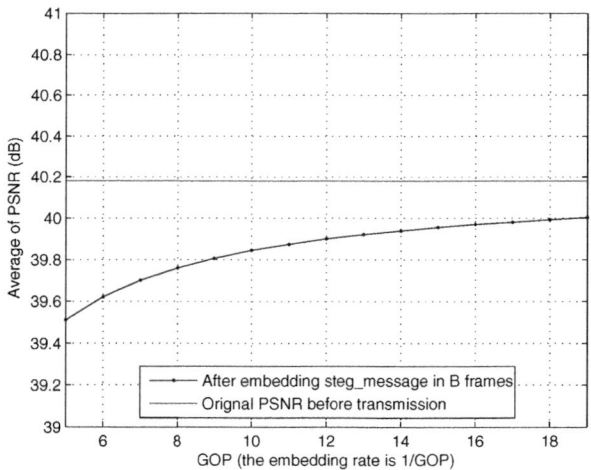

Fig. 12. Comparison of received video with original video quality at different insertion rate

If we decrease the insertion rate, for example to embed secret data in the first B frames in every 5, 6...19 GOPs, the received video quality could be improved. Fig. 12 shows the comparison of average PSNR of received video with average PSNR of original video before transmission, which are very close after the insertion rate is reduced to every 5 GOPs. Fig 13 shows the hidden channel bandwidth at different insertion rates. Note that for the smallest bandwidth provided in the proposed scheme 10.5 kbit/s, the received video quality is 40 dB, which is very close to the original PSNR 40.18 dB. The receiver cannot notice any quality degradation. The hidden channel bandwidth is 10.5 kbit/s, which is pretty high. For the maximum bandwidth provided by this scheme which is 199.4 kbit/s, the received average PSNR is 36.83 dB, which is still considered good.

We compare our proposed method with LACK [8]. LACK uses the lost audio packets to embedded secret data. LACK intentionally delays some audio packets to carry secret data. The effectiveness of LACK depends on the accuracy of the estimated mean call duration, the coefficient of variation of the call duration and the probability distribution of voice quality for the network which is intended to be used for sending steganographic data with LACK method [8]. Our proposed method is simpler than LACK. The secret data is just simply inserted in B frame packets and no statistical estimation of insertion time is needed; this algorithm could be implemented at the sender, or intermediate routers. The implementation is much simpler than the LACK. Note that the bandwidth of LACK and the quality degradation of voice transmission are not analyzed in [8].

Steganalysis to our proposed covert channels is hard to perform. Previously it has been shown that unusual traffic patterns may lead to discovery of covert channels. Our proposed covert channel does not change the traffic pattern, thus

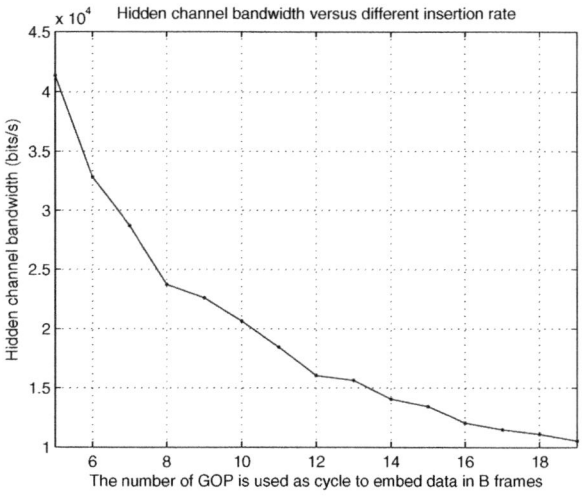

Fig. 13. Hidden channel bandwidth versus different insertion rates

it can not be identified by this method. Analysis of RTP packets which are already too late to be reconstructed at the receiver side could help detect this covert channel, but if we send the stego_RTP packets of B frames as normal packets as used in our proposed method, the covert channel cannot be detected. No real-world steganograhic method is perfect–whatever the method, the hidden information can be potentially discovered [8]. In general the more hidden information is inserted, the greater the chance that it will be detected. By analyzing the dropped B frame packets at the receiver side, the proposed covert channels might be detected especially if the insertion rate is high, e.g. the first B frames of every GOP in which the covert bandwidth is very high, and more data could be embedded. At the same time video quality will deteriorate. In that case our proposed covert channels can achieve video quality 36.83 dB, which is still considered good quality. Thus, simply monitoring video quality cannot identify our proposed covert channels. Analysis of dropped packets at receiver side could help detect the hidden channel. However, if we decrease the insertion rate, or decrease the bandwidth of covert channel, it would be harder to detect those covert channels as delayed packets are natural phenomena in IP networks especially during networks' rush hour. If the bit error happened in I frame packets, the impact would be severer than in B frame packets. The following Fig. 14 shows the lost I frame packets on video quality versus different channel conditions, which represent one bit error happened in every number of I frames (or GOPs as there is one I frame in each GOP), e.g. 5 represents that there is one bit error in one of 5 I frames, and 15 represents that in every 15 I frames there is one bit error happened in I frames. Because of direct and transitive dependencies, the entire GOP is lost when the I frame is lost. If one bit error happens in I frame the whole I frame will be lost and this dropped I frame packet will have impact on the following P and B frames within the entire GOP. Note that the

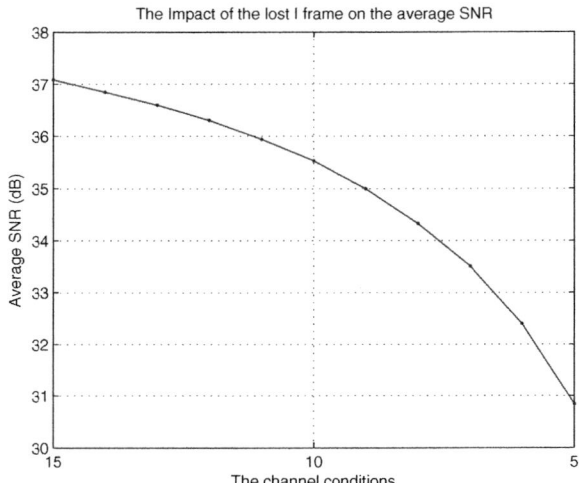

Fig. 14. The impact of the lost I frame packets on the video quality

average PSNR has been decreased greatly. For example if one bit error happened to the I frames of every 5 GOPs, the resulting average PSNR will be decreased to 30.8 dB. However, if the first B frames of every 5 GOP are used in carrying secret data, the resulting average PSNR is 39.5 dB. This covert channel cannot be identified by looking at the received video quality.

6 Conclusions and Future Work

The huge amount of data of multimedia applications transported over networks makes it ideal as a carrier for steganography. However, covert channels based on multimedia streaming has not been studied except covert channels based on VoIP. In this paper we propose new techniques to covertly transmit data via multimedia streaming. The proposed covert channel using SSRC and SEQ has no impact on received video quality. The simulation results show that stego_SSRCs and stego_SEQs have very similar statistical characteristics to regular SSRCs and SEQs, displaying randomness as required by standard. Thus, it is difficult to detect the hidden data by analyzing the statistical characteristics. This covert channel cannot be detected based on received video quality as it has no impact on video quality. For the proposed covert channel using RTP payload–B frames, the capacity and its impact on the received video quality are analyzed which has not been done in LACK. Simulations on real video traces are conducted and the results show the proposed covert channels not only achieve relatively high bandwidth but also keep the received video quality high. We also compared our method with LACK in terms of implementation complexity. Our method does not require statistical analysis of the carrier and thus is simpler and more practical than LACK. Furthermore our proposed method cannot be easily detected as it does not change the traffic pattern and still keeps the received video quality high.

In the proposed methods of hiding data in both RTP protocol and its payload–MPEG-2 frames, the unreliability of UDP is not taken into consideration. This will cause the loss of secret information when packets are dropped due to network congestion. It really needs some kind of measures such as error correct codes to make sure secret message can be completely transmitted, which will be our future work.

References

1. Szczypiorski, K.: Steganography in TCP/IP Networks. State of the Art and a Proposal of a New System HICCUPS. Institute of Telecommunications Seminar (2003)
2. Lioyd, P.: An exploration of Covert Channels witin Voice Over IP. Dept. of Computing and Information Sciences, Thesis, Rochester Institute of Technology (2010), http://www.tele.pw.edu.pl/~krzysiek/pdf/steg-seminar-2003.pdf (retrieved June 17, 2010)

3. Zander, S., Armitage, Z., Branch, P.: A Survey of Covert Channels and Counter-measures in Computer Network Protocols. IEEE Communications Surveys 9(3), 44–57, 3rd quarter (2007)
4. Forte, D.V., Maruti, C., Vetturi, M.R., Zambelli, Z.: SecSyslog: An Approach to Secure Logging Based on Covert Channels. In: Proc. First Intl. Wksp. Systematic Approaches to Digital Forensic Engineering, pp. 248–263 (November 2005)
5. de Graff, R., Aycock, J., Jacobson., M.: Improved Port Knocking with Strong Authentication. In: Proc. 21st Annual Computer Security Applications Conf., pp. 451–462 (December 2005)
6. I)ruid: Real Time Steganography with RTP, http://druid.caughq.org/presentations/Real-time-Steganography-with-RTP.pdf
7. Mazurczyk, W., Szczpiorski, K.: Covert Channels in SIP for VoIP Signalling. Warsaw University of Technology (2008)
8. Mazurczyk, W., Lubacz, J.: LACK– a VoIP Steganographic Method. Journal of Telecommunication System (December 2009)
9. Packard, H.: MPEG-2: The Basics of How It Works, http://www.home.agilent.com/upload/cmc_upload/All/6CO6MPEGTUTORIAL1.pdf
10. Hoffman, D., Fernando, G., Goyal, V., Civanlar, M.: RFC2250-RTP Payload Format for MPEG1/MPEG2 Video. IETF RFC2250
11. MacAulay, A., Felts, B., Fisher, Y.: IP Streaming of MPEG-4: Native RTP vs MPEG-2 Transport Stream. white paper, Envivo, Inc. (2005)
12. LIamas, D., Allison, C., Miller, A.: Covert Channels in Internet Protocols: A Survey (2005), http://gray-world.net/papers/0506-PGNET-Paper.pdf.
13. Mazurczyk, W., Szczypiorski, K.: Steganography of VoIP Streams. In: Meersman, R., Tari, Z. (eds.) OTM 2008, Part II. LNCS, vol. 5332, pp. 1001–1018. Springer, Heidelberg (2008)
14. Giffin, J., Greenstadt, R., Litwack, P., Tibbetts, R.: Covert Messaging through TCP Timestamps. In: Dingledine, R., Syverson, P.F. (eds.) PET 2002. LNCS, vol. 2482, pp. 194–208. Springer, Heidelberg (2003)
15. Schulzrine, H., Casner, S., Frederick, R., Jacobson, V.: RTP: A Transport Protocol for Real-time Applications. RFC3550
16. Jeffay, K.: The Multimedia Transport Protocol RTP. University of North Carolina at Chapel Hill (1999), http://www.home.elka.pw.edu.pl/ wmazurcz/moja/art/Eglobal_sip_covert.pdf
17. Lucena, N.B., Pease, J., Yadollahpour, P., Chapin, S.J.: Syntax and Semantics-Preserving Application-Layer Protocol Steganography. In: Fridrich, J. (ed.) IH 2004. LNCS, vol. 3200, pp. 164–179. Springer, Heidelberg (2004)
18. Seeling, P.: Video Traces for Network Performance Analysis, http://trace.eas.asu.edu/mpeg2
19. Software WireShark, http://www.wireshark.org
20. Zhao, H., Shi, Y.Q., Ansari, N.: Hiding Data in Multimedia Streaming over Networks. In: CNSR (8th Communication Networks and Services Research), May 11-14, pp. 50–55 (2010)
21. Cabuk, S., Brodley, C.E., Shields, C.: IP Covert Channel Detection. ACM Trans. on Information and Systems Security 12(4) (April 2009)

Author Index

GPSR Compliance

The European Union's (EU) General Product Safety Regulation (GPSR)
is a set of rules that requires consumer products to be safe and our
obligations to ensure this.

If you have any concerns about our products, you can contact us on
ProductSafety@springernature.com

In case Publisher is established outside the EU, the EU authorized
representative is:

Springer Nature Customer Service Center GmbH
Europaplatz 3
69115 Heidelberg, Germany

Batch number: 09490872

Printed by Printforce, the Netherlands